Leading Disadvantaged Learners

Also available from Bloomsbury

Collaborative School Leadership: Managing a Group of Schools,
David Middlewood, Ian Abbott and Sue Robinson

Mentoring and Coaching in Early Childhood Education, edited by
Michael Gasper and Rosie Walker

School Leadership and Education System Reform, edited by Toby Greany
and Peter Earley

Teaching in Unequal Societies, John Russon

Transforming Education: Reimagining Learning, Pedagogy and Curriculum,
Miranda Jefferson and Michael Anderson

Understanding Educational Leadership: Critical Perspectives and Approaches,
edited by Steven J. Courtney, Helen M. Gunter, Richard Niesche
and Tina Trujillo

Leading Disadvantaged Learners

From Feeling a Failure to Achieving Success

David Middlewood and Ian Abbott
with Roberto A. Pamas

BLOOMSBURY ACADEMIC
LONDON • NEW YORK • OXFORD • NEW DELHI • SYDNEY

BLOOMSBURY ACADEMIC
Bloomsbury Publishing Plc
50 Bedford Square, London, WC1B 3DP, UK
1385 Broadway, New York, NY 10018, USA
29 Earlsfort Terrace, Dublin 2, Ireland

BLOOMSBURY, BLOOMSBURY ACADEMIC and the Diana logo are trademarks of
Bloomsbury Publishing Plc

First published in Great Britain, 2022

Cover design by Charlotte James
Cover image © Ekely/Getty Images

A catalogue record for this book is available from the British Library.

Library of Congress Cataloging-in-Publication Data
Names: Middlewood, David, author. | Abbott, Ian, 1955- author. |
Pamas, Roberto, author.
Title: Leading disadvantaged learners : from feeling a failure to achieving success /
David Middlewood and Ian Abbott with Roberto Pamas.
Description: New York : Bloomsbury Academic, 2022. | Includes bibliographical
references and index.
Identifiers: LCCN 2021017355 (print) | LCCN 2021017356 (ebook) |
ISBN 9781350128286 (paperback) | ISBN 9781350128293 (hardback) |
ISBN 9781350128309 (epub) | ISBN 9781350128316 (ebook)
Subjects: LCSH: Children with social disabilities–Education--Cross-cultural studies. |
Academic achievement–Cross–cultural studies.
Classification: LCC LC4065 .M53 2022 (print) | LCC LC4065 (ebook) |
DDC 371.826/94—dc23
LC record available at https://lccn.loc.gov/2021017355
LC ebook record available at https://lccn.loc.gov/2021017356

ISBN: HB: 978-1-3501-2829-3
         PB: 978-1-3501-2828-6
         ePDF: 978-1-3501-2831-6
         eBook: 978-1-3501-2830-9

Typeset by RefineCatch Limited, Bungay, Suffolk
Printed and bound in Great Britain

To find out more about our authors and books visit www.bloomsbury.com
and sign up for our newsletters.

Contents

Preface

At the time of writing this preface, most of the world is still in the grip of an unprecedented viral pandemic. Like many other writers, our work has been interrupted by its drastic effects. In our case, we had completed our research, collated and analysed the data collected over a number of years during a number of projects, and were beginning to record the implications when the first lockdowns arrived! Thanks to the work and patience of everyone involved in publishing, we were later able to resume and complete the book.

The topic of the research was one that has concerned politicians, sociologists, educationalists and economists across the globe – the consistency of inequality between the prosperous and the poor. Specifically in education, this inequality relates to the way that those from secure and comfortable circumstances achieve so much more than those from more disadvantaged and deprived ones. As has been clearly stated:

> Wherever you look in the world, in Tokyo or Finland, Britain or Bulgaria, from Venezuela to Morocco, the picture is clear that children from affluent homes out-perform those from poorer homes. *(Bloom, 2012:3)*

This educational inequality, often referred to as an 'achievement gap', has severe implications for the future development of whole societies and whole nations. Whereas there was perhaps a period in the twentieth century when a belief existed that education in itself might be the panacea to a country's economic and social problems, it eventually became more widely and realistically recognised that education as provided in schools could not be separated from social issues of poverty, health, social housing and basic human necessities. It is an extreme irony that our research which tried, as others have, to ascertain some ways in which this gap could be narrowed or possibly eliminated for at least some learners, should be interrupted by something which has actually made the situation worse! We already know that the school closures and family isolation caused by the pandemic have adversely affected poorer children and families so much more than more affluent ones, thus potentially widening the gap rather than narrowing it. Prior to the pandemic, it had already been suggested that closing this gap might take a decade in developed countries such as the United Kingdom; now, even that prediction may look optimistic!

Because of these unique circumstances, this preface is necessarily longer than usual and several points need to be made.

This book is not and could not be about the pandemic; no doubt many books will be written in the future on this topic but, as explained, our research was completed just prior to this. We did manage to contact some of these we had previously interviewed to ascertain their early responses to its impact and these responses are included. What the pandemic has already revealed even more in various countries is the highlighting and accentuation of the inequality in educational attainment between those in disadvantaged circumstances and those from more prosperous contexts. It also seems to have emphasised even more the inadequacy of online learning compared with face-to-face learning, especially for those disadvantaged learners.

Whilst it can be argued that the word 'disadvantaged' is somewhat negative in a world that seeks to be more inclusive, we have retained the word throughout as we believe that it is currently very widely used and understood in the debate about the achievement gap. Also when we refer to closing the gap, we of course mean it in the sense of narrowing the gap, because, as already noted, the actual closure of this gap may be decades away.

The research that we carried out was in fact through a variety of separate research projects over a number of years, all officially funded and supported. Most of these were specifically centred on the learning of children in disadvantaged contexts, and a small number took place in recent years where we visited a country for teaching purposes and, whilst there, obtained permission to add to our data by interviewing various relevant school leaders and teachers and students. In those circumstances, we adopted identical research protocols to those used in the other projects. Overall, these projects included:

- four separate projects in a major English city – funded by its local authority
- two separate projects, one in an urban and one in a rural area – both funded by local authorities in England and Scotland
- three projects in South Africa – funded by English and South African Universities
- projects in Ethiopia and New Zealand – funded by the British Council
- project in Tanzania – funded by a state government
- three projects in Seychelles – funded by home national government and the World Bank
- two projects in Greece – both funded by local universities and the European Union

In all cases, the research involved visiting schools, studying relevant documentation, and interviewing key personnel – as noted above. This research has contributed to a number of publications, see for example: Abbott (2015); Abbott, Middlewood and Robinson (2013); Abbott, Middlewood and Robinson (2015); Middlewood (2019); Middlewood and Abbott (2015 and 2017); Middlewood, Abbott, Netshandama and Whitehead (2017); Middlewood, Abbott and Robinson (2018).

All this is to place the contents of the book in context, and we believe our findings and suggestions remain relevant as never before if those supporting, teaching, leading and managing learners and their families from disadvantaged and deprived circumstances are to be able to help turn failure to success. Our starting point was the recognition that, despite the inequality and its depressing impacts, there were and always have been notable exceptions. Even in the most deprived and disadvantaged contexts, a number of individual schools with their leaders and staff managed to achieve remarkable results and set their learners on successful life paths. In the truest sense, these were exceptional schools with exceptional leaders and exceptional staff. How was this possible?

As we were in the process of writing this book the Black Lives Matter movement gathered momentum, highlighting the multifaceted issues arising from race and disadvantage. Because the inequality between schools and learners manifests itself mainly on the gap between rich and poor, our focus has been on that aspect of disadvantage – material and financial deficit. We have placed less emphasis on race and ethnicity or gender, for example, whilst recognising its significance, because our research base probed those of different gender and of many different ethnicities, as the reader will see from the many case examples in the book.

Our research in various countries focused primarily on such schools as these (although we also saw many less successful ones of course), trying to ascertain whether there were aspects of their success which were relevant elsewhere and therefore whether we would be able to offer suggestions to other schools and staffs. Part One deals with the background to, and reasons for, the various inequalities that create the gap. After Chapter 1 has set the scene internationally for what is a world-wide phenomenon of a gap between rich and poor, Chapters 2 and 3 discuss in detail the various causes of the disadvantages that so many children and families face.

Chapters 4 and 5 examine the implications and ultimate consequences of the attainment gap and the inequality that is inherent in it, from the broader perspective of societies, countries' schools and systems, and also from the perspective of those families concerned and the schools they are involved with.

Part Two is concerned with what can be done about all this. Chapter 6 suggests our four key principles under the headings of leadership, collaboration, staff development and community involvement. Each of these is then explored in a separate individual chapter (Chapters 7 to 10).

We had been very pleased to accept an offer from Roberto to contribute a chapter (Chapter 11), giving a detailed case study of a school's success in the United States. This study embodied exactly the application of our key principles, arrived at quite independently by that author. This chapter adds a valuable perspective to the research.

Part Three tries to summarise our conclusions. The short answer to the question of how the gap can be closed and all schools succeed as these ones do, is that there *is no magic formula*! There is no single school system or structure or style that is guaranteed to offer any kind of blueprint for such success. To say this is not in any way to offer a defeatist outlook. Research has often shown that good ideas that work in one context are not easily transferred to a different context. This applies both at national level, where the intention of various countries to copy the 'Finland Model', for example, have been shown to fail, simply because the culture, history, core beliefs and societal structures of one place are unique to that place and cannot easily be replicated, however powerful the educational ideas are. Similarly, at school, as some of our interviewed school leaders – and teachers – found, what works in one school very effectively may fail in another, even where the two contexts appear alike. As we suggest strongly in our final chapter, the key to success is to apply key principles in the way that is appropriate to the specific people in the specific community.

Whilst there is in various places clearly a need for radical changes in educational systems, including use of resources, we found that the successful leaders for example, whilst often being very critical of the particular system in which they operated, spent little time bemoaning their fate. Likewise, we have focused here on what is achievable at a local, even a parochial level because that is where schools operate in trying to serve their local communities. There is little in this book therefore in terms of ideas at a global level to close the gap. Like the leaders and staff that we have seen achieving wonderful results, our concern has been for the learners that these people had in front of them *now* and their task was to succeed with them all, not wait for things to change! What underpinned the work of these successful schools, however appalling the contexts, was the belief that the leaders and staff had and instilled in everyone, a belief in:

- themselves
- their learners
- what they were doing and
- the value of education

With such belief and the actions arising from it, it seemed almost anything was possible!

When the pandemic is over, we believe these will still lie at the heart of future success.

We should like to thank all the people who have assisted us in this work and it has been a privilege to meet so many inspiring people of all ages, races and dispositions. As well as being grateful to Roberto, we warmly thank colleagues at Bloomsbury, and also Trish Caswell for her work with us and for compiling the index. Our personal thanks go to Jacqui (from David) and to Deb (from Ian) for their support throughout.

David Middlewood and Ian Abbott

Part One

Disadvantaged Learners: Causes and Consequences

Chapter 1
The Context of Disadvantage and Underachievement in Education

Introduction

This chapter describes and examines the widespread nature of the educational gap between the achievement of those from disadvantaged backgrounds compared with those from more favourable ones. It describes how the situation and outcomes for underachievers at school and college have become a major issue for many countries in this century as globalisation and the growth of technology increasingly affect all sectors of society. As Scheicher (2013: 4) has pointed out: 'It does not matter if you go to school in Britain, Finland or Japan students from privileged backgrounds tend to do well everywhere. What really distinguishes education systems is their capacity to deploy resources where they can make the most difference.' This will involve consideration of national education policies, the structure of individual education systems and economic, social, political and cultural aspects which can all play a part in developing and/or perpetuating the educational gap.

There is a need to explore both the micro and macro contexts of policy as governments around the world seek to address the causes of the gap and the implications and outcomes of the continuing differences in the educational achievement of young people from different backgrounds.

In this chapter we describe, discuss and explain the widespread nature of the educational gap between the achievement of those from disadvantaged contexts with those from more favourable backgrounds. This chapter therefore:

- considers the reasons why there are differences between the educational achievement of young people
- identifies the role government and national education, social and economic policies play in developing and or perpetuating the gap
- discusses some of the policy initiatives that have been introduced in an attempt to reduce/eradicate the gap
- explores the impact that individual schools and teachers can have on closing the gap

Reasons for Differences in Educational Achievement

All governments are striving to improve their education systems and to raise levels of attainment for each individual student for a variety of reasons. These include social, economic, political and fairness considerations. Over time there may be differences in the importance of each of these reasons depending on different priorities, but they will also play a part in determining particular policies designed to reduce educational inequality. For example, economic factors such as ensuring a highly skilled and productive workforce, which will enable a country to compete internationally may be the driving force that leads to specific policies which reduce educational inequality. Ensuring that all students enter the labour market with the highest possible skills level should provide opportunities for young people from disadvantaged backgrounds to enter professions they were previously prevented from entering.

Education is viewed as a significant factor in fostering social mobility and improving the life chances of individuals. However, in many countries there are significant differences in outcomes for different categories of young people. Individual governments will try to address these differences through a variety of policy interventions often directed at individual schools who have the final responsibility to implement policy. It is important to recognise that not all governments will give equal weight to fostering social mobility. There is also no agreed set of policy measures across countries to bring about social mobility, and inevitably politics will play a part in determining particular policies.

There are numerous reasons put forward to explain why there are differences in outcomes for different groups of young people. There are no hard or fast rules, there are factors that make it more likely that a particular student will perform less well in education. Some ethnic groups will outperform others, girls may do better than boys, children who have English as an additional language may initially struggle in the UK education system and may never catch up. In addition, the type of school and the catchment area, children in care, teaching quality, the availability of successful role models, home environment, parental income, standards of housing and health may all contribute to less successful educational outcomes. Students with Special Educational Needs (SEN) are also likely to perform less well in a formal education system, although this may be down to a failure on the part of the education system, schools and individual teachers to recognise individual difficulties. The picture is complicated and there is no guarantee that children from a particular group, in a certain type of school, from a disadvantaged background will perform less well in education. There are many examples of children from what would be described as a deprived background obtaining positive outcomes from their education. Generally, however, students from a more advantaged background tend to do better in education in terms of outcomes which in most systems is in terms of exam results. It is important to remember that measuring outcomes in education can be difficult. Should it just be about exam success or should we consider, for example, wider factors such as happiness, the ability to make a positive contribution to society, being an effective citizen or a broad understanding of the arts?

Many of the differences between groups of children are in place before they start school. Exposure to a broader range of language, a range of educational experience, the availability of books, positive life experiences, a more stable home background, better diet and health will all give a young child a head start as they enter primary education. Schools have a responsibility to compensate for some of these issues, but in some cases, it is difficult to sustain this as the circumstances of individuals can and do change over time.

Case Example 1.1

An experienced (15 years) headteacher of an outstanding secondary academy school in the north-east of England we visited as part of our research, attempted to explain the context of the school by describing the case of two students:

'We have a very mixed student intake. Part of our student intake comes from a fairly affluent part of the town and we also have significant number of students from what can only be described as run down and very challenging in terms of socioeconomic problems, poverty unemployment, crime etc. Our primary schools do a great job in making up for some of the home problems experienced by some but not all of our students from the less affluent areas. We aim to continue that work and we are careful not to categorise students. There are some really support-ive parents across the board. However, let me talk to you about Poppy and Honey. They came from the same primary school, with broadly similar Key Stage 2 profiles, both very bright and committed. We continued with our programme of support for Honey who was from what we would describe as difficult home circumstances. A lack of parental support and involvement is a polite way of putting it, a really dysfunctional family, school was a safe place for her. As she went through Key Stage 3 and 4 these problems became worse with ongoing police and social service involvement. There were frequent absences and she really struggled to take part in school. We put a lot of support in and she did manage to get a reasonable clutch of GCSE passes, but nowhere near her potential. She went on to college, but dropped out after a year. Of course, Poppy, from a much more settled and affluent background faced none of the same problems, got top grades at GCSE, did exceptionally well in her A levels and went to medical school. I'm not down-playing Poppy's achievement, she got what she deserved for her hard work and commitment, but Honey had the same level of ability. Of course it shouldn't be all about exam success, we kept Honey safe and free from harm, she didn't go hungry, we gave lots of pastoral support to her and her family, but at the end of the day it's the exam grades that we are judged on.

I suppose some would consider what we did for Honey was a success, she could have fallen out of the system earlier, and she has something to build on, but I feel it was such a waste of potential. Those two always stick in my mind when I'm talking about these issues, how difficult it is for the school, could we have done more? However, we should not lose sight of the fact that we do have many students who come from equally tough backgrounds who do go on to succeed, it's just that I hate to see potential going unfulfilled.'

Case example 1.1 illustrates some of the practical issues involved in attempting to close the gap. A wide range of factors can intervene and derail the hard work and commitment of education professionals. The school has an extremely positive reputation for its work with disadvantaged young people and is successful in overcoming many of the disadvantages they face. In Honey's case, from the school's perspective, they were only partly successful and it is important to remember that school and teachers are not the only factors that impact on educational achievement, happiness or well-being. A complicated mix of issues such as home circumstances, environment, peer group, housing, family attitudes, will impact on young people as they grow up and influence a range of outcomes. A legitimate stance could be that the school actually did well and without their intervention things could have been much worse for that particular student.

As we were writing this book, the world was faced by a major pandemic which forced whole countries to close down their economies and enter prolonged periods of lockdown. In many countries, schools were or have been closed for many months and individual students received little or no formal education. In many education systems, face-to-face tuition in schools has been replaced by online learning. This is an attempt to mitigate the loss of schooling, but again it is likely that better-off families with access to technology, a quiet space to work in and supportive parents will adapt to this new way of working better than those from disadvantaged backgrounds. Once a significant period of schooling has been lost it is very difficult to compensate for this form of disruption. The COVID-19 pandemic therefore is likely to make the gap even worse and to disadvantage the already disadvantaged even more. This is especially true in developing countries which often lack basic infrastructure even when times are good. The impact on most nations' health across the world has been clear to see, with climbing rates of infection and high mortality rates. We are also starting to see the economic, social and increasingly political impact of the pandemic. McCoy (2020: 13) has claimed that: 'Ultimately the government won't be judged by the health effects of coronavirus alone. The fallout from the pandemic will be felt socially and economically, entrenching inequalities that already exist in our society.' Analysis early in the pandemic in England has estimated that:

> School closures will make the attainment gap between disadvantaged children and their peers grow, likely reversing the reduction in the gap achieved since 2011. The median estimate indicates that the gap would widen by 36% . . .
>
> It is highly likely that the gap will have widened when schools return to school, even if the strongest possible mitigatory steps are put into place . . . it is unlikely that a single catch-up strategy will be sufficient to compensate for lost learning due to school closures. (Education Endowment Foundation, 2020: 4)

The onset of the COVID-19 pandemic disrupted the public examination system in many countries with end-of-course examinations being cancelled. The use of estimated grades based on the use of norm referencing generated controversy with claims that students from disadvantaged backgrounds were being unfairly discriminated against. In Scotland the devolved government decided to overturn the original grades that had been awarded and base the final grades on teacher assessment (BBC, 12 August 2020). In England the government originally decided against the course of action and retained the original grades, which penalised many students from disadvantaged backgrounds, but were forced to backtrack following a public outcry about the unfairness of the system and the lower grades awarded to disadvantaged students and schools from poorer areas. Patel (2020) claimed that: 'the exams result system – like so much of our society – is not designed to be biased but it reflects and exacerbates the inequality and injustice that blights so many of our communities'. In this book we are not specifically concerned with issues surrounding the examinations system and the award of final grades, but the COVID-19 pandemic has highlighted many of the inequalities that exist in education systems and it is the poorer members of society who tend to suffer the most. As Benn (2020) has pointed out: 'This year's exam results won't just shatter individual confidence in the system – they will confirm that this system disadvantages the already disadvantaged at every turn, despite its official rhetoric about closing gaps and improving social mobility'.

There are also substantial inequalities between countries who will be facing different sets of challenges. Whilst education professionals in any system will never be satisfied about the absolute level of resources available, there will be relative differences between countries. In richer countries there will be issues around how resources are deployed, in poorer countries there may be a shortage of basic resources. However, in either case the issue is about how best resources can be used to address differences in educational achievement. We will return to this issue in later chapters, but it is easy to recognise the differences when a country does not have the level of resource to provide basic facilities for education and class sizes are 60 compared to a richer country which has a relative abundance of resources and class sizes are no bigger than 25. The problems faced by the poorest nations are likely to be much greater in scale than more developed countries with a significant majority of young people underachieving and, in some cases, failing to get even basic access to education. There are different issues about levels of achievement for students if a system as a whole is failing, compared to a system where one group is failing to achieve its potential.

The causes and impact of inequality are a major area of concern for government, society, families and most notably for individuals in many countries around the world. These inequalities manifest themselves in a number of areas including income, health provision, housing, social care and education. These are usually interconnected and lead to similar outcomes for people in different countries. Fewer employment opportunities, lower incomes, poorer health, increased social problems, a greater likelihood of involvement in crime and reduced life expectancy are all potential outcomes of inequality that is often passed from one generation, despite government intervention, to the next.

This is not to say that every person from a disadvantaged background will not succeed in education for the rest of their life. We have to be extremely careful not to confirm stereotypes, and to acknowledge that many people from poorer backgrounds will succeed in education. There will also be a group of people who do not do well in formal education systems, but who go on to have happy, successful and worthwhile lives. As education professionals we can occasionally lose sight of the fact that education is not always a significant factor in determining future achievement or well-being for everyone. We have all seen examples of individuals who have not done well in formal education but who have gone on to successful careers in a range of occupations. However, for a significant number of people who do not do well at school their life chances will be severely reduced and they will find it difficult to make progress in terms of employment opportunities and income. There are a large group of young people who fail to reach their potential due to a failure to perform well in formal education. As a consequence, governments around the world accept that education is a significant factor in improving the life chances of many young people and has a key role to play in promoting opportunities to overcome disadvantage.

Social Mobility

Many of the policies we will examine later in the book will be concerned with encouraging and enabling social mobility. In particular, improving the educational and employment prospects of an individual relative to their parents (Smith, 2018). An example of this in practice would be a young person gaining access to higher education and achieving a university degree, whilst their parents left school at the statutory leaving age and did not go on to achieve further qualifications. In the United Kingdom a number of organisations have been set up to increase social mobility. For example, the Sutton Trust was established in 1997 to 'fight for social mobility from birth to the workplace so that every young person – no matter who their parents are, what school they go to or where they live – has the chance to succeed in life' (Sutton Trust, 2020). The Social Mobility Commission was established by the central government to: 'monitor progress towards improving social mobility in the United Kingdom and promote social mobility in England' (Social Mobility Commission, 2020). They define social mobility as 'the link between a person's occupation and income and the occupation and income of their parents. Where there is a strong link, there is lower social mobility. Where there is a weak link there is a higher level of social mobility (Social Mobility Commission, 2020). Another example of a charitable organisation trying to improve the life chances of young people in the United Kingdom is the Social Mobility Foundation, which was founded in 2005 and aims to: 'provide opportunities and networks of support for 16–17-year-olds who are unable to obtain them from their schools or families' (Social Mobility Foundation, 2020).

Other organisations have been set up to deal with perceived specific problems in the education system, which are deemed to restrict the life chances of individual students. In the United States, for example, Teach for America works with: 'children growing up in disenfranchised communities who lack access to resources and opportunities and attend schools that are not equipped to meet all their needs' (Teach for America, 2020). According to the National Centre for Education Statistics (NCES) '1.3 million students drop out of high school in the United States. More than half are students of color, and most are low-income. Students from low-income families drop out of high school at the rate of upper-middle- and high-income families' (NCES,2018). Teach for America recruits 'a diverse network of leaders who confront educational inequality by teaching for at least two years in a low-income community (Teach for America, 2020).

An example of a similar type of organisation in the United Kingdom is Teach First which was set up to reduce 'educational disadvantage and to raise the status of teaching . . . whose vision is that no child's educational success is limited by their socio economic status' (Abbott, Rathbone and Whitehead, 2019: 120). Teach First trains teachers and recruits their trainees from leading universities. The trainees agree to be placed in schools that serve economically disadvantaged communities. The purpose of this approach is to provide the opportunity for school students from disadvantaged backgrounds to improve their levels of academic achievement and also 'raise the teaching standards of those who teach alongside them in the same department' (Abbott, et al, 2019). We will return to the issue of teaching standards and professional staff development in Chapter 9.

There are many other organisations involved in trying to improve social mobility and we can only give a flavour of the range of approaches here. At this stage we are not making any judgements about the effectiveness of the different organisations or the approaches they are promoting to close the gap. No one should doubt their motives and the individuals involved in these organisations are genuinely committed to improving the life chances of young people. However, the establishment of a large number of organisa-tions and initiatives gives an impression of the importance given to the drive to improve social mobility. There is a veritable industry of government bodies and charities, in many countries involved in this type of activity. Despite being long established, with large amounts of resource and extremely well-intentioned individuals, the problem of relative educational underperformance of a significant minority of young people persists. We will return, later in the book, to look in more detail at some of the strategies employed by organisations to increase social mobility, especially the role of schools and teachers.

Case Example 1.2

Oxford University aims to recruit outstanding undergraduates whatever their back-ground. The university has targeted their outreach activity at potential students which are under-represented at Oxford, including:

- students living in neighbourhoods where there is low-participation higher education (POLAR)
- those living in areas of socio-economic disadvantage (ACORN)
- schools with little history of successful Oxford applications
- under-represented ethnic minority groups (African, Caribbean, Pakistani and Bangladeshi)
- first-generation HE participants
- women in science, technology, engineering and mathematics subjects (STEM) subjects
- white working-class boys and girls
- rural and costal locations with a history of low progression to higher education

There is an access and participation plan in place with targets for some of these groups. In addition, the university is developing a bridging programme and a foundation-year programme for students from state schools from under-represented backgrounds. The overall aim of this initiative to increase the particip-ation rates of students from a range of backgrounds and to:

- raise attainment in schools and encourage applications to selective univer-sities;
- encourage and support applications to Oxford from students from under-represented groups and
- ensure fair opportunities for admission

The annual amount of resource to support these initiatives is slightly over £4 million (Oxford University, 2020).

No one can doubt that the programmes of Oxford and other leading universities to support students from disadvantaged groups are worthwhile and an attempt to address long-standing issues of unfairness. They will help a number of individual students and provide them with the opportunity to attend a world class university. Central government in the United Kingdom has recognised the issue of access to leading universities and has put pressure on them to have an access and participation plan approved by the Office for Students. Without these plans these universities would not be able to charge fees above the basic level. Our issue is not with the initi-ative, which is of obvious benefit, but the emphasis given to it as a significant policy to improve social mobility. We will argue in Chapter 12 that individual initiatives are important, but that systemic change has to take place if the attainment gap is to be closed. These types of initiatives will lead to improving life chances for the minority, but do little to deal with the underlying causes of the educational gap. However, it is important to be realistic and to accept that system-wide change is not within the grasp of most individuals, and as educators we have to do the best we can for the young people we work with in the circumstances we are working in. As a consequence, a range of schemes are warmly embraced by educational professionals.

Different Solutions, Markets and Systems

In a significant number of countries since the 1980s, the dominant ideology relating to the way in which the economy and society operates has been market based. The emphasis has been on giving individuals choice and introducing competition. Put simply there is a belief that competition will force standards to rise, and those providers who do not offer what consumers want will eventually go out of business. Therefore, it is in their own self-interest to keep raising standards. This has been the case in some areas of the public sector, for example health and education, as well as in the private sector where the consumer is given the opportunity through the market to obtain maximum satisfaction from the goods and services they buy. If you are not satisfied with your mobile phone from one company, switch to another; if your local school does not offer what you want for your child's education, choose another school or even set one up yourself. However, individualisation will not necessarily maximise societal welfare. Providing equality of opportunity does not necessarily lead to everyone getting the same outcomes. A whole range of factors will intervene, from a lack of knowledge to markets operating unfairly through the use of cartels or price fixing. In terms of closing the gap, giving everyone the opportunity to succeed is not the same as actually achieving it. Some of the factors we identified earlier in the chapter mean that all children do not start on their educational journey equally and during that journey circumstances can and do change. We have already highlighted issues such as home, background, parental support and type of school that may mean that a child is already starting out with considerable disadvantages. Despite the emphasis on a market-led system there has been a growing realisation that governments have to intervene to deal with a range of issues and the market has to have some form of regulation and control.

In education we have seen the development of a quasi-market (Le Grand and Bartlett, 1993). A quasi-market has a number of similar features to a free market and competition between schools and colleges is encouraged to drive up standards. However, the state will intervene in the market to maintain consistent standards in areas such as curriculum and assessment and to protect groups of students who might otherwise be disadvantaged. As a consequence, governments will introduce policies that provide some specific form of support for particular groups to level up opportunity. An example of this is the introduction of the Pupil Premium in England which allocated additional resources to schools to be used with students from disadvantaged backgrounds. We will return to look in more detail at this policy later in the book, but schools were allocated higher levels of funding per pupil that could only be used for a range of activities and support for particular students and not across the school as a whole. Whilst this type of policy and additional level of support is valuable for individual students, it can only go so far in addressing some of the underlying causes of the gap. It will not be able to bring about system-wide change. Countries such as England, the United States and Australia have experienced enormous change in their entire education systems as they have embraced the market, but the attainment gap still remains.

Perhaps an emphasis on the market is not the solution? Within any market-based system there will be winners and losers. We have considered how the state can intervene and mitigate this to an extent by providing additional support for particular groups, but the belief remains that marketisation will inevitably raise standards. As an alternative, greater central and local control of schools and an emphasis on co-operation and collaboration with an end to the unfair allocation of resources might be worth considering. A practical example of this in practice might be to remove or reduce some of the advantages that certain groups or individuals receive. It would be completely unfair to undertake this in the case of individuals, but it could be an option within a system. For example, removing or reducing the advantages of private or selective schools might free resources for other parts of the system and lead to a greater focus on disadvantaged students to make education provision more equal. However, reducing the education performance of a relatively high achieving group will not necessarily lead to an improvement in the performance of more disadvantaged students. The attainment gap might be reduced but that might not lead to improved outcomes for the more disadvantaged or society more widely. This is a decision that has to be made by policy makers who have to judge the impact on the system as a whole and to consider the wider implications for society. Whatever system is in place our view is that it has to be designed to give every young person an equal opportunity to achieve their potential and to provide choices for that individual, it is schools and their teachers who will be at the forefront of this process.

Schools and Teachers

We have considered a wide range of issues and briefly looked at different policy interventions designed to close the gap. However, in practice, it will be schools, their senior leadership, teaching and support staff who have to deal with the actual implementation of particular policies. All schools will attempt to do their best for their students, but that is not to say that all outcomes are the best. In practice there are significant differences between schools and teachers. There are some schools that are coasting, whilst others are performing well in difficult circumstances. Even good schools can have relatively poor teachers and not every good teacher will be able to motivate all students. Within and across schools there are many factors that have to come together to coordinate policy and lead to a significant reduction in the attainment gap. A number of internal and external issues will impact on schools and teachers:

- level of resourcing including staffing numbers
- external school structure, type of school
- physical location of the school
- quality of facilities and space
- school leadership and management
- staff training and development
- staff commitment
- behaviour policies
- setting and streaming policies
- pastoral support for students and families
- parental support
- community support

- assessment policies
- curriculum content

Schools and teachers cannot work in isolation and it is important to remember that many of the causes of poor performance in education are outside the control of the school. That is not to make excuses for the performance of schools, but to recognise that social and economic problems, such as low-quality housing, poor diet, family break-up, domestic violence and low incomes, which contribute to poor educational performance cannot be solved by schools or teachers. They require sustained and significant social intervention to address them. However, schools and their teachers can mitigate the effects and help to reduce the size of the educational gap.

Conclusion

In this chapter we have considered a wide range of issues relating to the educational gap and the role played by the state, schools and teachers. We have identified a complex mix of factors that contribute to the existence of the educational gap and given some examples of specific initiatives that have been introduced in an attempt to reduce the gap. We recognise the reality of having to work within the system that is already in existence, but we have put forward some alternative approaches that could impact more broadly on policy. However, in the rest of the book we will focus more on specific school and college-based experience based largely on our own research in those institutions. We will be putting forward a number of approaches that can be utilised by schools and colleges. In the next chapter we will consider in greater detail who are the disadvantaged learners.

Summary

This chapter has:

- considered some of the reasons why there are differences between the educational achievement of young people
- identified the role government and national education, social and economic policies play in developing or perpetuating the gap
- discussed some of the policy initiatives that have been introduced in an attempt to reduce/eradicate the gap
- explored the impact schools and teachers can have on closing the gap

Chapter 2
Who are the Disadvantaged Learners?

Introduction

This chapter describes the various contexts in which children and young people encounter deprivation and disadvantages, which, as well as having hugely negative impacts on their lives and development, greatly influence their ability to achieve in education. Specifically, the chapter:

- examines the impact of poverty on households and families, and its implications for the children concerned
- discusses some of the circumstances which can disrupt or destroy families' ability to function 'normally'
- considers the extreme circumstances of children in a post-conflict or post-tragedy situation and the impact on them
- compares and contrasts the motivation of children emerging from an extreme situation with those living in perpetual 'low level' disadvantage
- draws attention to the parallels and differences between disadvantage in urban, rural and other settings, with their implications for children's schooling

Poverty and its Impact

For what is known as absolute poverty, the United Nations' 1995 definition clearly states that it involves severe deprivation of basic human needs, including food, safe drinking water, sanitation, health, shelter as well as education and information. This situation often applies to those in desperate situations in undeveloped societies, whereas relative poverty is often found in the more deprived sectors of more developed countries and societies. This involves the deprivation of not only material resources but also access to services and other aspects of civil and social life, or – as Townsend (1979: 13) describes it – exclusion from 'ordinary living patterns, customs and activities'. This notion of social exclusion has gained credence since the 1990s and also led to the use of the word 'underclass' as a descriptor of those who are permanently dependent on government benefits and thus unlikely to be empowered to achieve economic stability or self-sufficiency. This can lead to them being seen as 'a potential threat to social and economic stability through criminal activity, drug use and relative social and political powerlessness' (Parrish, 2010: 272). In this book, we are concerned specifically with education more than the wider societal issues, but there seems little doubt that those families and their children from the contexts being described here can unwittingly be seen as a threat to the status quo in various schools in particular neighbourhoods, not just because they may automatically be viewed as likely to have an adverse effect on the school's academic performance (as measured in exam results), but because they represent an undesirable distortion of the school's 'normal' way of being. Teaching being primarily a middle-class occupation, it is perhaps unsurprising that some teachers tend to view middle-class pupils and parents more positively than working-class ones, about whom they may hold rather stereotypical ideas (Dunne and Gazeley, 2008). As we discuss later in the book, educational staff, like social workers, need to be able to appreciate the complexities of learners' environments rather than view their difficulties and the way in which these are manifested in school as reflecting personal or family failings or inadequacies. Stinson and Wager (2012) stressed that teachers needed above all to have local knowledge of the students' contexts and particular cultural and social issues relevant to them.

According to figures from an independent source, in the United Kingdom, a developed country, there are about four and a half million children (of the 14 million children in total) living in poverty in 2018 (Family Resources Survey and HBAI dataset). In the United States, 22 per cent of children under the age of 18 were identified by the US Census of 2013 as living in poverty. Even in apparently stable areas in the United States, such as Maryland, in over a third of its schools, the number qualifying for free lunches increased by 20 per cent in the first decade of the twenty-first century (Orfield, 2002). In the United Kingdom, single-parent families are twice as likely to be in poverty as couples with children. In this context, one of the significant developments of the second decade of the twenty-first century is how the percentages of those households in poverty actually have someone (or two) in paid work, but are still unable to feed or clothe their families adequately. Whilst unemployment is still a huge factor in causing poverty in many developed countries (Greece and Spain in Europe for example), this new trend is notable as an indicator of the need to constantly update any stereotyped thinking about poverty. Families may in some cases be juggling with several jobs in order to make ends meet. The growth in the need for food banks in the United Kingdom (and several other developed countries) and the way the demand for these increases during school holidays (when school lunches are not available of course) is another indicator of family struggles. There is an irony in terms of the educational implications of such things in that teachers themselves may be among those struggling to pay their bills and there are recorded examples in the United Kingdom of teachers having to use food banks, apply for loans from teacher welfare sources, and buy goods in charity shops. Such is the widespread use of food banks now in countries such as United Kingdom that even a reading and picture book for young children illustrating everyday life makes reference to visiting them regularly (Milner, 2019). An OECD (2016) report noted that similar problems for teachers were occurring in Greece and Spain.

Examples of basic items being unavailable in poverty-affected households include toothpaste, bedding, clothing and girls' sanitary products. This last mentioned gives a clear example of how the simple provision of such products can restore 'some dignity to schoolgirls, by allowing them to attend school all month', according to the founder of Freda, an online retailer of sanitary products which donates free products to a project which delivers them to schools. In the United Kingdom, different governments have recognised this problem and have given money for the purchase of girls' sanitary products, with Scotland doing this in 2018, Wales in 2019, and England in 2020. This loss of dignity which living in poverty can bring can also arise, for example, from being unable to pay for the funeral of a family member, or a pregnancy test, or access to other services. Two other factors may be mentioned here, such as the actual fear of poverty being as debilitating as much as poverty itself. This fear can lead to excessive borrowing and resultant debt, whilst the other factor is the amount of time spent in poverty, highlighted by Gorard (2018). Whilst some families can experience temporary hardship, perhaps even poverty, in, say, periods of unemployment, much more serious is the perpetual struggle over many years to put food on the table and provide basic necessities. Over 12 per cent of the United Kingdom's total population is seen as in 'persistent poverty', meaning that those people have spent the last four years without basic necessities (Family Resources Survey and HBAI dataset, 2018). The effects of such living are discussed later. Whilst we refer to households, it is important to remember that a significant number of children, both in developed and developing countries, have no actual 'home' at all in any physical sense. In the United Kingdom, only 40 per cent of the 130,000 homeless children in 2011 attended school on anything like a regular basis (Cundy, 2011), and even these inevitably suffer from lost sleep, no suitable places to do homework, and of course the feelings of insecurity caused by such instability.

Related Disadvantages

As has already been indicated in this book, many of the inequalities in societies tend to go together, so that 'an individual who is disadvantaged in one area of life is likely to be disadvantaged in others' (Scambler and Blane, 2003: 111). The link between poverty and poor health for example is well established. The diet of the low paid is more likely to contain far less fresh fruit and vegetables and more cheap 'ready made' meals which contain more salt and sugar than that of the higher paid. Although it is undoubtedly true that major health concerns in wealthy economies this century involve over-indulgence in high sugar content foods and simple excess consumption, leading to worries about heart disease and diabetes for example, it is a fact that such high-earning households have a choice in their consumption, whereas the choice for low earners is very restricted. The health consequences of poverty can start before birth with poor nutrition often leading to low birth weight, whilst normal early childhood development can be inhibited by poverty, and poor hygienic facilities can increase the risk of various infestations. The experience of Adam, interviewed for this book, is a striking example of the inter-relatedness between an upbringing in relative poverty and setbacks in education.

Case Example 2.1

Adam, now in his mid-fifties, is a respected employee in an English university. He was born into a poor family with an unskilled labourer father and living in a run-down urban area, where the houses have long since been demolished. He recalls the house being very damp, with primitive washing facilities. Adam said: 'I suffered from breathing problems from an early age and missed quite a bit of schooling at primary. In the secondary school, I complained regularly that I couldn't hear the teachers properly, but I think it was generally thought that I was a slow learner, whose absences had kept me behind others. It was not until I was about 14 years old that I had my hearing properly tested and I was found to have a significant hearing problem which was actually noted as "partial deafness" caused by a chronic ear disease. To cut a long story short, this was eventually found to be linked to my "upper respiratory tract infection" which had, according to my specialist, been mostly attributed to the damp home conditions I had lived in for virtually all my childhood and youth.'

Once Adam was fitted with the appropriate hearing aid support (completely invisible to the naked eye today incidentally), he made remarkable 'catch-up' progress at school, securing respectable passes at 16 plus, then passing his Advanced Level examinations at a local further education college, two of them at top grades. More than 30 years later, Adam holds a responsible position in higher education, specialising in Special Needs Education. He told his interviewee that one of the main reasons that drove him to enter the career world of SEN education was his concern that there were children living in poverty and poor health who might not be as fortunate as himself in having their problems recognised and diagnosed and thereby being forced to lose out on opportunities such as he then had.

Of course, poor health is by no means limited to physical health. In developed countries this century, there is considerable concern about the mental health of children and young people, with countries such as Japan expressing concern about suicide rates among teenagers; and in the United Kingdom, a report from a House of Commons health and social care committee noted that around one in ten children are living with some form of diagnosable mental health condition and, markedly, the poorest fifth of households are four times more likely to have a serious mental health difficulty than those in the wealthiest fifth (Committee Report, 2018).

A high proportion of those households in poverty in countries such as the United Kingdom are likely to contain a disabled person. The implications for a disabled child in terms of schooling are perhaps more obvious and are discussed in Chapter 3, but where the disabled person is an adult, especially a parent, the consequences for children's schooling can be huge. Notably in single-parent families, the child may be forced to be the carer for the disabled adult, which means the investment of enormous amounts of time, energy and commitment on the part of the child, quite apart from missing out on recreational activities with friends and classmates. Becky, a primary school teacher in a London Borough, told us of four cases (three girls and one boy) in a single class of 10- and 11-year-olds where she, with the help of staff teaching assistants, found the child was responsible for the care of a parent. Becky was alerted to these situations by the persistently late arrival at school of these children, by their falling asleep in lessons in two cases, and general high anxiety and nervousness in behaviour. In one case, Becky found that one of the girls was stealing other children's food from their bags for a younger sibling, because the mother could not leave the house to shop and the girl and did not have enough time or money to buy at the shops herself. In all these cases, social welfare workers were eventually informed, and the situation eased somewhat. In two of the cases, considerable opposition had to be overcome from the mother and child because of the fear that such involvement might mean the child or children being removed from home into the care system.

Other factors which significantly affect behaviour and performance at school include domestic abuse, whether physical, sexual or emotional. A study by a charity of young people who were homeless in one city in the United Kingdom found that a high percentage of them left their homes between the ages of 14 and 16 because of domestic abuse by an adult. In nearly all the cases, their time at school had suffered greatly because of the abuse and the need to be secretive about it, feeling unable to share the problem with school staff or social support workers, because of the shame brought on themselves and/or the family, or the belief that nobody would believe them.

Drug misuse, gang culture and its pressures, violence and child trafficking are additionally all issues that demand extensive description and investigation which are not possible here. Some of these are in no way necessarily related to poverty or lower income contexts (violence and drug abuse can occur at any level of society), but where they do exist, the pressures on children and young people are clearly enormous and can easily relegate education and schooling to a very low place on the scale of importance to such families.

Tragic Occurrences

The extremities of disadvantage brought about by armed conflict and huge natural disasters such as earthquakes are beyond the scope of this book. This is a field of study in its own right in terms of the impact on children's education (see, for example, O'Donoghue and Clarke, 2019). However, the indirect effect of such circumstances can and does impact in dramatic fashion on schooling in countries totally unrelated to the original tragic event. The dire consequences of physical warfare on civilian populations lead many citizens to flee their home countries in desperation and seek a home elsewhere. Thus, in this century, unprecedented numbers of families and individuals have escaped to try to find refuge in more stable countries and the issue of emigration/immigration on a large scale is one of the major concerns of our time. If one adds the need to escape from poverty and exploitation, the reliance in many cases on illegal 'traffickers', and the loss of life during the journeys, it is obvious that many of those children that do manage to arrive in a new country and enter the educational system there begin with massive disadvantages. Again, the scale of this is too large for it to be considered in depth here, but schools in developed countries, especially in European countries and in North America, face these challenges. Furthermore, because such incoming migrants often tend to settle or be placed in specific areas, the pressures often fall on specific schools which consequently may have large numbers of such children. Typically, such children, or their whole families, may have no knowledge of the native language of their new country, adding to the problems facing their teachers and school leaders. We were privileged to be able to interview a small number of immigrant children – and some staff – in Crete, to where a number of families from Syria, Afghanistan and Libya have fled. The story of Jason, now a 13-year-old boy, is enlightening.

Case Example 2.2

Jason interviewed as a lively, intelligent boy with a keen sense of humour, tending to the mischievous side, leading us to envisage him as a 'handful' in class! He told of his journey in a boat across the ocean from Turkey, his family having fled from Syria when their house was destroyed by bombs. He has been in Crete six years and still sees a counsellor on an occasional basis. He conversed comfortably in English for the interview and was interested in learning new words from us! He has also learned Greek since his arrival, as well as his native tongue of Arabic, and told us that he would like to learn German soon. He attends the school for teaching English where we interviewed him, after mainstream school, and loves it there because of the pressure that is put on him to achieve – 'I like it because they make you do well, and if you make a mistake, you have to learn to put it right'.

He said he gets bored very easily in some lessons in secondary school and gets into trouble because of that. He makes friends quite easily now and has typical ambitions of wanting to be someone important in society later on.

Such has been Jason's progress at this school and his grasp of English so developed, that he took the role of Oliver in that school's Christmas production of 'Oliver!' in 2018!

Clearly, Jason was fortunate in that he undertook his awful journey and settlement in a strange land with his parents, whereas many children arrive as immigrant orphans. However, his current success shows what may be possible for those in such extreme disadvantage, and the head teacher of that school is referred to in Chapter 7 on School leadership and management.

Other occurrences may not be as extreme as post-conflict migration, but can equally destroy normal life as families know it. What is known as the major economic crisis which began in 2008 affected many families in various countries, who had been relatively stable in terms of income until that time. In one school in Crete, we were told of John, whose family had lost everything around 2010–11. From having a secure and well-paid job, John's father now existed on various poorly paid part-time jobs, with his mother doing likewise. They had lost the house they owned and had moved several times from one rented accommodation to another. Fortunately, John had at least remained in the same schooling area, as had his two sisters. The school was aware that John had no changes of clothes and his mother was assiduous in washing and repairing the one shirt, jacket and trousers he possessed. We were told that John was extremely bright and should definitely go to university after the secondary school which he now attends. One teacher said, 'He is a delightful boy, with good manners and a lovely sense of humour. He has no outdoor clothing, and when it rains or snows, he can miss some days at school, and he is fiercely loyal to his family, so we have to avoid any kind of patronising him'.

Referring to Canada, Abdi (2014: 84) points out an interesting contrast between children from families which have been accepted as legal immigrants and those who have arrive through dire necessity as refugees: 'in the case of Canada, immigrants who are chosen on a points system that includes education, specialised skills and language proficiency will be better endowed in the schooling possibilities of their children than refugee families'. This is something which would be relevant to many other countries.

Clearly, there are many thousands of children and young people who have suffered from a drastic change in financial circumstances which places the family in at least relative poverty, sometimes temporarily, sometimes permanently. The closure of a major employer in an area which has been dependent on its existence for its livelihoods is an increasingly common occurrence, especially as heavy industries contract. One relative consolation in these cases may be the sense of community that often emerges when many local people are in the same situation. Schools can often play an important role in community cohesion here. Chapter 10 on Community involvement gives an illustration of this.

Mike is a principal of a secondary academy in a town in the north-east of England, which once relied on ship-building at the nearby city docks for its employment and prosperity. He told us, 'When I came here, not long after the last ships had been built and the docks closed, there was a huge air of defeatism in the community which rolled over into the school. Everyone was saying, 'What's the point?' to everything. Students, with a very few exceptions, didn't see the value of learning at school because it wouldn't lead to anything. Parents had everyday struggles to survive and I have never known anything like it. There were actual suicides in some homes, people moved away, and nobody expected things to get better. It was depressing to see some students, especially boys, who were intelligent, just not bothering to do work at school because it all seemed pointless. It is a little better now, but the area has never recovered and at school, it is a long battle for all the staff to achieve much.'

One of the interesting things about the viewpoint expressed here is that it does possibly link with an issue that educational researchers and sociologists have noted in the United Kingdom – the relative underachievement of white working-class children (especially but not exclusively boys).

Emma is the principal of a primary academy in a town in the East Midlands of England. The town was formerly an important industrial and manufacturing base but, like many others in the twenty-first century, has declined in prosperity. She described her school's area as 'mainly white working-class' with moderate levels of unemployment. Jobs were generally low paid, and often both parents worked, although there were quite a large number of single-parent households. The attitude of many of her households towards school and education generally was that it was of limited value, although 'individual parents mostly say they'd like their child to do well at school!' Emma and her staff felt that this outlook was based primarily on the parents' own poor and often unhappy and unsuccessful experiences of their own schooling. (This generational aspect of underachievement at school is explored in Chapter 5 later in this part.) She noted that parental engagement with the school was 'poor' and this was an area the school was working hard on improving. Although the number of immigrant and minority ethnic children was small in the school, it was interesting to note that she and the staff found that the few non-UK born children had parents, such as those from Poland and Lithuania, whose engagement with school was 'good'.

Two other things may be worth noting about the children and families in this kind of school and community. Many families were in receipt of various state benefits but, according to Emma, they tended to lack any kind of financial understanding, 'as if they never expected it to be any other way. A kind of helplessness, even haplessness – "that's the way it is" sort of outlook.' Emma and her staff, as well as the trust of which her school was part, were all firmly committed to helping families to improve this, at least for the next generation, through their children. Some of what Emma as leader attempted is returned to in chapters in Part Two of this book.

The second feature mentioned by Emma was the lack of coherence in the community, often epitomised by parents arguing with each other – 'I know it shouldn't be said of course, but I wonder sometimes that at least if they all ganged up against the school on something, there would at least be some kind of harmony! These arguments between parents are ones begun at home, between neighbours for example, and then just carried on into school playgrounds and even reception area.' Emma had been very daunted by such things when first appointed, but now was determined to change things. (Again, see later chapters.)

Schools in deprived areas with high intakes of white working-class children seem to receive weaker inspection reports than those with a high proportion of migrant children. In an interview (House of Commons, 2015), the Chief Inspector of Ofsted noted that these white working-class communities had suffered the full brunt of economic dislocation and can therefore lack the drive and aspiration of many migrant communities. But we suggest the problem goes beyond that, to what has become an ingrained sense of hopelessness after what can be two or more generations where parents have been unable to tell their children that if they work hard they will 'get somewhere'.

Once again, underpinning the attitude that affected the underachievement of children here is the lack of motivation for doing better at school. Motivation is essentially about purpose, and many children living in perpetual deprivation see no point, or very little point, in tasks or targets they may be set at school. Certainly, long-term aspirations which may depend on school success to be fulfilled may seem of little relevance to someone whose immediate concern is whether there will be anything to eat when they get home, or in even worse circumstances whether some form of violence can be avoided/frustrated at home. If motivation is defined as 'to be moved to do something' (Ryan and Deci, 2000: 54), then it is this 'moving' that is the school's biggest challenge, in situations where not getting any worse may sometimes be seen as an achievement. The further problem, according to Bush and Middlewood, 2013: 113), is that motivation is a highly individual process, so that attempts to 'move' people in any group sense are unlikely to be very successful. For example, a policy that says, 'We will do so and so for all our white working-class boys' is unlikely to work because each of those boys is a unique individual, whilst having of course some things in common with others in the grouping. Thus, not only is each learner individual, but each context in which they operate is so also. This special nature of context is what we turn to next in this chapter.

The Special Nature of Specific Contexts of Deprivation and Disadvantage

Inevitably, as we ourselves have done already in this book, generalisations about the issues of deprivation, poverty, disadvantage and so on have to be made, and of course policies at national and regional level work in this way by their very nature. However, it is important to be aware that the factors affecting these issues will vary according to context. Here, we wish to note that different kinds of physical, social and geographical contexts mean that the individuals or groups there will be affected in different ways. For example, it is common practice and understandable to distinguish between urban and rural poverty in terms of the different impact these will have on disadvantage in each context. In reality, the term 'urban' can cover widely different places, from highly densely populated large cities to towns with populations of little more than ten thousand people. Many people in city suburbs live in communities larger than this, and some towns have populations larger than the smaller cities. One principal of a primary school in such a small town in the north of England described that town as very 'inward-looking, and almost resentful of outsiders'. She described how her predecessor as leader had always tried to appoint teachers who were 'as local as possible, and had been to training institutions for teachers as near as possible to this place. She was very proud of this by the way!' Similarly, in rural communities, settlements range from villages as large as small towns, to hamlets with a handful of dwellings, and some individual dwellings can also be several miles from the next one.

It is also worth mentioning that in England, the inspection authority Ofsted has drawn special attention to coastal communities as a further example of contexts of specific deprivation and disadvantage. This primarily is where such coastal towns were formerly thriving and prosperous seaside resorts for holidaymakers, but, as fashions changed, they became economically poor without visitors, and considerable deprivation occurred. Our research did not include this particular context, but its existence underlines that simplistic divisions into urban and rural are inadequate and also how circumstances beyond local people's control can quickly change circumstances in which they live and schools operate.

Also, the nature of specific locations will change over time. In the United States, the nature of suburbs in many cities has evolved in a way that strikingly affects its people and their schooling. The increase in diversity in city suburbs in the 1980s led to increases in poverty levels (Lucy and Phillips, 2000). By the early twenty-first century, suburbs, especially those closest to the cities, were experiencing many of the problems associated with cities, such as poverty, segregation and deterioration of public services. This created a snowball effect, as more prosperous families moved to outer suburbs and problems grew in the inner suburbs as professional expertise, family stability and buying power waned, leaving a weakened societal existence (Casella, 2014). Monti (2004) claimed that suburbs that were once the hallmark of the American dream were now more likely to experience unstable housing prices, drug-related criminality, gangs, traffic and strains on public services. According to Casella (2014, p. 191), children in these contexts are 'growing up in a society with great disparities of wealth that affects their learning'.

Of course, this changing of the character of an area is not uncommon in developed countries where the marketisation of education has led to more affluent families moving to gain access to schools seen as being higher performing. The movement of higher achieving children to schools in 'better' areas has meant that schools in abandoned areas come to be seen as weaker and the areas as poorer. Thus, the division between the two types of schools increases and is perpetuated.

Focusing specifically on rural deprivation and disadvantage, we can note that one of the biggest factors affecting people may be isolation from others. The sheer distances between villages or even dwellings make community cohesion much more difficult. In many countries, both developed and developing, many small village schools have disappeared, and pupils therefore may have considerable distances to travel simply to get to school. Public transport services in rural areas, such as buses or minibuses, are, even in developed countries, likely to be the first to be reduced when budgets are restricted because, compared with towns, their provision is uneconomic. Attendance at rural schools is inevitably more problematic, and any attempts to follow up absentees becomes an almost impossible task for those concerned, because of the distances involved. One local authority officer in a predominantly rural county in the east of England abolished all its posts for education welfare officers (who dealt with school attendance) in 2010 because of the travelling costs involved. A deputy principal of a large secondary school in a Midlands town whom we interviewed about community issues had previously worked in a school in that particular authority. She noted the difference in that in her current school there were support staff who would visit the homes of non-attendees to work with families. She herself raised the comparison that, in her previous rural and widely scattered community where 80 per cent of pupils came to school by hired buses, it was impossible to make such contact with pupils living in the farthest villages, despite awareness of deprived circumstances at home. She said, 'Although we did manage to reach and help a few of them, we were well aware that there were several more we could not – it was heartbreaking, to be honest'.

Among other disadvantages faced by rural schools may be that of teacher quality. An OECD report (2018) noted that there were significantly higher numbers of 'less qualified' teachers in rural schools than in urban ones in countries such as Turkey and Kosovo. In many developing countries, this was also true on a significant scale, and as Bolat (2014) noted, when attempts were made to compensate for this by increasing the number of teachers, the problem was actually accentuated. It is also likely that qualified teachers may often prefer to work in towns or cities where they may have done their teaching practice and where they feel more comfortable. Of course, there are many excellent teachers working in rural schools in many countries, and indeed, as Brock (2011) noted, teacher innovation can be thriving there because teachers are driven onto their own resources when remote from outside sources. Nevertheless, rural and remote schools do suffer from distinctive disadvantages, as well as many of those faced by schools and children in urban areas.

Among their research projects, the authors of this book carried out an investigation into the leadership of schools in rural communities specifically in two states of South Africa, one of them being the most deprived state of that country. Obviously, this initially included analysis of the rural context of the schools concerned and it is helpful to describe the features of this context here (Middlewood and Abbott, 2017).

Many rural communities here exist in isolation and a weak infrastructure means that virtually all roads are untarred and difficult to use in bad weather – flooding makes them impassable at times. Some villages lack adequate sanitation and water supply is erratic. Rural poverty is widespread. The isolated nature of these communities and the absence of amenities that modernity has brought to urban areas mean that many people remain inward-looking, believing themselves to be neglected or ignored by the powers that be, whether regional or national. Believing they need to be self-reliant to survive, village elders still retain considerable influence in some communities, with links with other villages seen as desirable only if beneficial to that community. Some of the consequences for schools include:

- poor attendance (in one state, there is a high dropout rate after primary education is completed with some pupils having attended very little schooling by that time – especially girls)
- teacher absenteeism – most teachers live miles from the schools, and even a routine matter will involve the teacher visiting an urban amenity, leading to absence from work
- theft and vandalism – in some villages, the school is seen as having more resources which are valuable, and is therefore a target

- lack of resources – not only in terms of libraries and computers, but also basic writing equipment
- teacher numbers – teacher training in South Africa is very urban-centric, and very few trainees do any actual teaching practice outside of the towns, so that teachers are very unprepared for rural conditions
- relatively poor quality of actual teaching and learning – with a reliance on rote learning and teacher monologue. Latest developments seem unlikely to reach isolated communities and their schools.

It is worth drawing attention to the fact that there are virtually no recorded examples of significant unrest in such rural areas, unlike poor urban townships, where uprisings – including violent ones – against living conditions have been seen. Possible resentment against conditions is exacerbated by the visible existence of relative prosperity in the nearby urban areas. This absence of protest may be evidence of a certain 'passivity and helplessness of outlook towards their situation' (Faulkner, 2015: 424). This particular outlook of children and communities and its consequences are considered in more detail in Chapter 3.

The way in which school leaders set about tackling the issues raised through this context is shown in Chapter 8 on Collaboration.

Conclusion

The circumstances of deprivation and disadvantage in which many school learners exist are many and various. These may be temporary circumstances for some, but for many others, this may be a persistent state from which they see little prospect of emerging or changing. The conventional view may always have been that education is an escape route, and there are many stories and examples of individuals achieving this of course, and going on to attain high status in society. For the majority, however, the reality is that schools are unable to do this at present. The reasons for this are addressed and examined in the next two chapters.

This chapter has:

- described some of the impacts of poverty on households and families, with the implications for the children involved
- discussed some related circumstances which prevent such families from functioning normally
- considered the extreme circumstances of families in tragic situations, such as post-armed conflict
- compared and contrasted the outlook and motivation of children in those extreme situations with those in perpetual low-level disadvantage
- pointed out the various different physical environments, such as urban and rural within which deprivation can exist and take different forms

Chapter 3
The Causes of Disadvantage and Underachievement

Introduction

This chapter examines the ways in which the disadvantaged contexts described in the previous chapter often manifest in the school performance, behaviour and progress of the children from such contexts. Specifically, the chapter:

- details some of the patterns of personal circumstances that have a negative impact on schooling
- considers the wider implications of this in terms of lack of opportunity and under-fulfilment of talents
- discusses how the inevitability of being a 'failure' at school follows for many children, and the implications of this

Patterns of Daily Circumstances

The previous chapter described the various contexts of disadvantage in which some children exist. It particularly emphasised poverty and hunger, ill-health and related issues which impact hugely in a negative way on their education. But what is it actually like for children and their families to live in poverty for example, and what part does schooling play in such lives? How are schools perceived by such children and their parents?

Talking with staff who work in schools with large numbers of children in impoverished homes, one is often struck by the commitment of many who deliberately chose to work there because of their compassion and zeal for improvement. Sometimes, this is because they themselves came from poorer backgrounds and have a driving desire to help other similar children. However, one also meets individual teachers and support staff who, although knowing of 'unfortunate' and 'poorer' children, only become fully aware of the reality of the children's circumstances when they encounter the pupils on a daily basis. Some become totally shocked and begin to understand this reality for the first time. Teachers are intelligent people, and in general they are people who read and can filter the media. They will therefore usually be aware of the figures for poverty in developed countries, for example, and this may influence the way they vote in political elections. If they come from reasonably comfortable middle-class homes, as many if not most teachers do, they can be relatively unaware of these realities initially. As those intelligent people, school staff are aware of poverty, disadvantage, and deprivation, and find this shocking but, like many things in life, only when faced with the actuality of these in the behaviour and outlook of the children seen on a daily basis does the reality of what these words mean hit home perhaps.

Karen, now in her late thirties, provided a useful illustration in her interview:

I moved here (to a city in Eastern England) when my husband got a promoted job in the area. I am not overly ambitious for myself and enjoy being a good – as I think I am! – classroom teacher. I applied for a job (as a teacher of 11- to 13-year olds) here and got it straightaway. I knew it was a poorer area of the city, originally a London overspill area, I was told, and thought it would be a new challenge as I had previously only worked in very affluent or conventional middle class places. It certainly was a challenge! I nearly gave up at the end of a fortnight! I saw the behaviour as terrible (not hostilely rude but indifferent), attendance was poor, children were late to lessons, and most of them didn't seem to be able to concentrate for more than a few minutes. After I'd been there about a month, I complained to a senior teacher about the behaviour and non-attendance and failure to do homework of Luke, a 13-year-old boy. This head of year – a very wise person it turned out! – said that Luke's mother happened to be coming in to see her that day so would I like to join them?

That meeting opened my eyes! The woman who came in was apologetic about Luke and explained several things about his life, some of which the head of year had clearly heard previously. She did not complain or whine, but described how she had visited a food bank that morning, had waited three hours at the benefits office, and had had to keep Luke off school the previous week for one day as she had no one else to care for her two-year-old while she attended her own hospital appointment. Other things involved hiding in the house while debtors called for money she owed which she had borrowed for her father's funeral! I now cannot remember it all, but I know that I never saw Luke – or those like him – in the same light again. I went home to my own comfortable house quite guilty after that, but realised that didn't help anyone of course. My attitude changed and I know I became a much better professional teacher after that.

Karen's school is described in Chapter 10 in this book, as is Karen herself as a now successful teacher!

The brief insight into Luke and his mother's daily life that Karen received is perhaps a useful illustration of what many families and their children in disadvantaged circumstances face. In their lives, school is inevitably less important than several other more pressing things which helped them survive through life's necessities. School to them could not be said to be a necessity!

Some children have daily experiences that are as difficult as those of Luke, and the following two examples show these.

Case Example 3.1

The situation of Shelley, a 14-year-old girl, was given to us by her head of year at the school she attends in a former mining town in the North West of England.

'Shelley has reeled from one crisis to anther ever since she joined us at the age of 11. I looked at her primary school records and they were not too bad, but something happened, I think, round about the time she changed schools. Most of her friends went to another school and she felt isolated here. She got into bad company outside of school, has been arrested twice for shoplifting – petty goods of no great value. She has been to juvenile court, therefore. Her social worker told me she turns up for meetings and is always promising to behave well. She comes late to school and truants from some lessons, but her behaviour is not too bad at school. Hers is a single-parent family and she seems to get money from somewhere – I fear the worst about where the money comes from! She is not anti-school as such but is totally negative about her future, her prospects, and is very aggressive if you suggest she could do well. Once she blurted out, "What's the point? What's my life going to be like? I don't want to end up like my mum, with nothing nice to wear and can't go anywhere. I'll find a way out!" I could not get any more out of her, but it sounded ominous!'

Case Example 3.2

Karim is a 12-year-old boy of Asian descent in his second year at a secondary school in a town in the Welsh Borders. The town – and the school – has a mix of reasonably affluent students and those from much more impoverished homes, of whom Karim is one. The deputy principal of the school told us that: 'Karim is currently suspended from school for stealing money from another boy's coat, then using it to buy his own lunch. When he was accused, he at first denied it but later admitted it, saying he was so hungry as he had not eaten for about 30 hours – which I am sure was true. The trouble is that while he is out of school, he won't be eating again, I suppose. We did not really want to exclude him, but the parents of the boy he stole from kicked up such a fuss and said they'd take their son off to another school if we did not take tough action. (Their own son did not make that fuss, by the way!) If I'm honest, I think the school felt it could not afford to lose students like that one and if he left, others might follow! Personally, I felt there was a racial element to it from those parents as well, but I could be wrong of course. We have all sorts of ideas about how to help Karim when he returns, but we have to be sensitive and not appear to be patronising in any way. I am optimistic. Karim is quite a bright boy and has real talent in art and design. We'll work on that. I know that nobody in the family is in work, and, because only one parent speaks English and that not too well, I wonder if they get the benefits they may be entitled to. Things are difficult and I'm going to ask a welfare officer to look into it – tactfully! There are four other children at home, I know. Karim was bullied a little bit when he first came here, but that all settled down.'

There are many more extreme cases that research can show about the circumstances in which schoolchildren exist outside of school. These two Case examples, however, give insights into how living in households where there is poverty impacts on learners' attitudes and outlooks, which the schools may struggle to combat. Shelley's 'ominous' (according to her teacher) determination to do better than her parents by some means that does not involve doing well at school, and Karim's being driven to theft and therefore being excluded from school both illustrate this vividly. As far as can be ascertained, neither story involves such issues as drug-taking, sexual abuse, or violence. Rather, they seem to show the debilitating effects of living in a setting of perpetual low-level poverty and disadvantage. Our third Case example now illustrates something slightly different.

Case Example 3.3

We interviewed the head of sixth form in a large school in the South West of England. The school is in a city which is largely prosperous and is regularly reported by the media as the 'best place to live in England'. However, it has its pockets of poverty and disadvantage, such as the one where Karen lives. Karen is in her first year of sixth form and the interviewee spoke admiringly of her. 'I think that for her to get the four GCSEs she did was a tremendous achievement. Although that is below the level we normally set for access to doing Advanced Levels, I and other teachers argued strongly for her to be allowed to do them. She loves history and has a real feel for it – I think she'll do well at that. When I think of what she has had to go through, compared with some of our other children, who get private tutoring, can go on skiing holidays, and pay for dance classes and so on, she is a marvel!

For five years here, she has been the family carer (we now have a younger sister here three years younger); her dad works night shifts in a warehouse packing parcels for one of these big international companies and he comes home in the morning, wakes Karen, who then makes the breakfast for the family. Her mother is slightly disabled, not enough to claim benefit, and goes off to do part-time work in a nearby shop. So they both work, but this is a very expensive place to live in and I know that it has been a struggle all the way. She has never had a holiday, and during school holidays, Karen has worked in various cafes since she was 14. Her clothes are all second-hand and she is extremely tired lots of the time. She can't join any school clubs because of needing to get home and yet still manages to do her homework – most of the time. She deserves to go to university to do history, but whether she will be able to, I don't know. We will certainly try to help her!'

Karen's family's situation is what has become known in developed countries as that of the 'working poor'. Once being poor was seen in developed countries as being related to being out of employment, but in this century many families struggle to feed and clothe their children and themselves, despite either one or both adults having paid work. Additionally, of course, this work is in jobs that are mostly poorly paid, perhaps part-time, temporary, with unsocial hours and often what is now known as part of the 'gig economy', that is with no security and only being called upon when work is available to the employer. Sometimes the parents may have two or three such jobs, and still only just manage to fund a life of bare necessities. In these situations, apart from the lack of actual food and clothing, there will be very little time to allocate to 'normal' child interaction and, of course, physical exhaustion is a common complaint.

As shown in Karen's situation (Case example 3.3), some children will succeed against these odds, supported by schools and their staffs. The tragedy is that even someone like Karen who so courageously achieved what she did could have achieved so much more if she had been able to access a wider offering of educational opportunity. While children from most households use the internet and various forms of social media without giving it a second thought, the founder of the world wide web, Tim Berners-Lee (2020) pointed out that in the United States an estimated twelve million children live in homes without any broadband connectivity, and in United Kingdom, sixty thousand children have no internet at home – 'poverty stops many more from learning online when schools are closed'. (The 2020 closure of schools due to the COVID-19 pandemic provided stark evidence of this.) Karen's inability for example to join any additional clubs or enrichment activities was mentioned by her teacher, and it is to this that we now turn.

Lack of Opportunity and Under-Fulfilment

The curriculum in so many schools around the world, but perhaps especially in developed countries, is in this century very intensified in trying to provide everything that it is believed tomorrow's citizens will need to know and learn. With success in education being so linked by national governments with economic progress, the scope for nurturing creative talents becomes very limited. Whilst the importance of development in activities such as sport, design, the creative arts and performing arts has always been recognised as a part of personal development, they have often been offered through what are known as extra-curricular arrangements, such as clubs and societies, training and practice sessions. These are usually offered after the end of the official school teaching day, and, increasingly during school lunch breaks.

Research (Social Mobility Commission, 2018) showed that children from poorer homes in England were three times less likely to take part in after-school activities than other children. The reasons for this often included:

- Cost. This often included the cost of public transport – especially in rural areas – as pupils' bus passes were often not eligible for later travel. Also, further research by the Sutton Trust (2018) showed that children from poorer homes were more likely to participate in extra-curricular activities if they were free.

- Time. Many poorer children needed to get home quickly after school to undertake domestic duties, such as caring for a disabled parent or siblings, or collecting younger siblings from where they had been cared for during the school day (usually by a relation or friend or neighbour).

- Lack of equipment or kit. Most did not possess appropriate clothing such as sports footwear or a leotard for dancing.

Our own research into successful schools in disadvantaged areas showed that they had often initially had to help overcome other factors, such as the children's:

- Lack of confidence in their own ability. This tended to increase over time, as the older pupils were before they gained any experience of an activity, the more reluctant they became to believe they could be any good at it.

- Indifference to what was on offer. Similarly, some activities offered by schools were seen as esoteric and only for a certain type of person. Some sports which involved specialist equipment (such as tennis) were seen as middle class and inappropriate for them.

- Unwillingness to try something new. Security is often found in familiarity, and poorer children were less likely to be adventurous in trying something new.

- Fear of ridicule from other participants. This often related to inappropriate dress (as above), or perceived poor ability. There was, however, little evidence that any actual ridicule ever occurred.

The implications for children from poorer homes as described in the previous chapter, can be clearly seen in those systems where fee-paying schools exist alongside state-funded ones. For example, a study of the Charity Commission's register in United Kingdom in 2019 revealed that England's 30 most successful Parent-Teacher Associations (PTAs) of state schools raised over three and a half million pounds for their schools, with one school in North London raising nearly £900,000 and six others all over £100,000. In contrast, of the 30 schools with the highest proportion of children eligible for free school meals, only nine had a PTA at all, and the average raised was £1,700 (Ferguson and McIntyre, 2019).

Regional variations in England were also clear, in that 24 of the 30 successful fund-raising schools mentioned above were from London and the South East and none were in the North of England. Of the disadvantaged 30, most were in the North and just three in London. Similarly, in terms of music, only 9 per cent of children in the North East played a musical instrument, compared with nearly 23 per cent in the more affluent South East. One head teacher of school in an impoverished area of a city in the north of England told us that she had been trying to recruit a music teacher for two years without success and commented, ' I do understand that they might not want to come here when they see a woeful lack of instruments and no after-school clubs or concerts. It will take someone with what I call musical missionary zeal to take it on!'

Thus, in terms of extra-curricular activities, the opportunity for some schools to offer a vast range of creative and sporting activities is clear, whilst for their poorer counterparts, it may be hugely limited. Residential experiences, for example, will be impossible for children who have care responsibilities at home, quite apart from costs incurred that may be prohibitive. Thus, these experiences which a teacher in Abbott et al. (2015) quoted as being 'finding out that what they had daily was only part of life' are denied to them, leaving their daily routines as their only knowledge of existence. Lack of opportunity and potential for broadening horizons may not only occur through a lack of extra-curricular activities of course. In one primary school we visited in a medium-sized town in central England, known for its shopping facilities and its historic spa, the head teacher had carried out a survey on being appointed to the post. It showed that more than 40 per cent of the pupils had never visited any of the town's main department store, its public gardens, its cinemas, its spa centre, its swimming pool, the public library or local theatre. Moreover, about 25 per cent had never visited the adjacent town – it is literally adjacent in that its streets begin where this town's street ends. This school was in a poorer area of the town, receiving its intake from a large council housing estate built mainly in the 1950s and 1960s, and now somewhat dilapidated.

Given that opportunities for experiencing situations outside of an often-narrow daily routine are limited, the influences on the development of children in these circumstances are likewise restricted. School itself may be virtually the only one of these, and school visits, visitors to the school and 'out of the norm' activities can provide important insights into different feelings and ideas which stimulate children's responses. '. . . they can begin to realise that there can be a different world out there, and not everything is just like theirs. Above all, possibilities may begin to be seen for them!' (teacher quoted in Middlewood and Parker, 2009, p. 106). The successful schools visited saw these additional opportunities as fundamental to raising attainment and indeed did not really view them as 'additional', but an integral part of the child's educational experience at school. The crucial factor for poorer schools is that such activities are provided without cost to the pupil or family. Whilst there are examples in the second part of this book of schools discovering and nurturing talent through their offering of experiences, Case example 3.4 shows in a powerful way the waste that can occur.

Case Example 3.4

Carl was identified early in his secondary school life as a highly gifted gymnast. The principal of that school, in the West Midlands of England, said that his head of physical education had told him that he had never seen anyone so naturally talented as Carl. This was during normal PE lessons in the timetable, where gymnastics only took place for a six-week period, twice a year. The gymnastics club was available after the end of the school day, but Carl would have been the only boy – all the rest were girls – and he would or could not attend. The school offered to give him extra practice at lunch times but he said he had to go home at that time each day to check on his disabled mother. She was wheelchair bound. As a last resort, the school offered to enrol Carl with a local gym club and assist with the costs involved, using pupil premium funds. 'Local' in this case meant about eight miles away and the school offered to pay his travel expenses, with the club saying that it would take over that expense if he proved talented and committed. After much persuasion, Carl attended one session at this club where his outstanding talent was immediately recognised. In the end, Carl failed to appear for any future sessions and would later be absent from school on the day he was due to go to the club after school. The principal said: ' We tried to get to the bottom of it but I think that the family felt they could not manage without his daily support, and just wanted him to leave school as quickly as possible to earn and/or be at home full-time. The family was not hostile at all and said they appreciated our efforts but, in my opinion, were weakly dependent on him and did not have any long-term idea of a future for him or indeed for any of them. It was a tragedy in my view and I often think of him as the 'star that got away' through nobody's fault except what his life had condemned him to. It makes me angry to think of it! I don't know, I'm afraid, what happened to him as an adult; I can never get any news of him from anyone.'

One of the noticeable points about Carl's story is his lack of commitment, of course, and for people to succeed in sport clearly great commitment to continual practice is cited as necessary, as well as natural talent. How much can Carl be blamed for his lack of commitment to his development as a gymnast, compared with his enforced commitment to his family? It is a tragedy that he had to choose between the two. The schools which the pupils in these Case examples attended cannot be necessarily be blamed; we met many teachers, staff and teachers trying hard to succeed and doing so with several individuals, such as Karen (Case example 3.3). As one teacher, in an informal chat in the staffroom, put it: 'Every day is a struggle here, but if I can get some, even a few, of my group to succeed, it makes it worthwhile!'

Such determination is commendable, but it ought not to be the case that the others outside those 'some, even few' should not have a chance to succeed. Some schools seem to have found a way and we give examples later.

One of the wider implications of children like Carl not taking part in such activities is of course that for the country concerned, a huge amount of talent and ability is going unrecognised and unfulfilled, greatly to the detriment of that country's progress and heritage. There are unhelpful stereotypes about those who are successful in particular fields, and these can be off-putting to the next generation of aspirants, who look at successful people and may conclude that they cannot identify with them. Thus, both in the United Kingdom and the United States, concern has been expressed that students from certain backgrounds may not get into schools of drama. The chief executive of the Incorporated Society of Musicians in the United Kingdom has expressed a fear that 'music education is in a crisis, and the government must act quickly to ensure that music does not become the preserve of a privileged few' (quoted in interview in *The Times*, 6 July 2018). This can also be counted as an economic loss, since unfulfilled ability can mean not only unfulfilled human happiness, but also lost income. Moreover, taxes not paid by those who might have gone on to more demanding and more highly paid jobs means less wealth for any country.

Through a meeting at a research conference in the United States, we made a connection with Laura, an experienced teacher in New York. On the subject of out-of-class activities, she wanted to tell us of her own experience and sent us this scenario, along with prospectuses of the two schools concerned.

I have taught in several schools and in different boroughs of New York. It is an exciting place and I love its 'buzz' and some of its challenges. I have taught in schools in wealthy areas and in schools, which, frankly are bottom of the pile. The thing that always grates on me is how the students in the latter group miss out at all levels. Even when classroom ethos and teaching standards are not so bad – and in some places it is not so good! – the whole school experience can be negative, in the sense that after school, there can be nothing for them. In one school, everyone was too exhausted by the day's work to do any more, and I blame no one there. I felt the same! But when I thought of the school I had been at three years previously in a wealthy area, I felt a kind of despair. Those students had everything-a huge range of sports on offer for coaching and development, close links with notable sports clubs, and easy access to scholarships later on. Also, there were endless opportunities to play musical instruments, join choirs and groups, dance of every possible kind, and social events which increased confidence. I can't imagine how many promising footballers, athletes, musicians, artists, and so on are lost to the nation because you are not in the right place at the right time at that stage of life. I should have done more but at the time, I was too junior and too feeble perhaps.

The prospectus of the wealthy school included a section on famous alumni to attract parents and prospective students, thus perpetuating the cycle and the gap. Fortunately, there are schools that have succeeded in offering a rich range of activities to disadvantaged students and schools, both in New York and elsewhere – some are described in Part Two.

However, sadly, for many children living in the extreme disadvantaged circumstances such as have been described, going to school may be seen by them as something which has to be endured (because the law says you must go to school), or an irrelevance, or at best, something rating very low on a list of priorities in helping them to a tolerable existence on a day-to-day basis. *Unless* the school can demonstrate to them that it is something very important, something which brings some enjoyment into otherwise often gloomy lives, and, perhaps most significantly, something which gives them hope for the future, this is a view which can be readily understood. What is positive is that in the research carried out which led to this book were found many schools, led and staffed by outstanding leaders and teachers and support staff, that were able to do exactly these things. Part Two of the book (Chapters 7 to 11) shows how they did this.

A Sense of Failure

Given all the various circumstances described already that many children exist in throughout their compulsory school years, it is probably inevitable that many of them leave school with negative feelings, both about schooling and more significantly perhaps about themselves. First, since success at school in most countries is often measured by the number of passes and good grades achieved in public examinations, so many children from poorer homes fare much worse overall than others. Thus, these school leavers are unlikely to win awards, receive glowing testimonials from school or have their names in school registers or records of achievement. Statistics from 2016 showed that, excluding the 'extremely poor', just one in three children from lower-income families reached the UK government's target for GCSE passes, whereas more than 60 per cent of students from middle class families did so (Antonucci, 2016). The reasons for this lower attainment include several factors already discussed, such as poor attendance at school, inability to attend extra sessions (such as after-school revision classes in the final stages of courses), no possibility of paid extra tuition which is available to children from wealthier homes, and inability to do normal homework and coursework because of inadequate facilities at home, thus causing some children to under-perform. Exceptions do of course occur, as our Case example 3.3 showed with Karen, and many others, some with outstanding results.

However, in some ways, this sense of failure caused by a weak final set of examination results is less important than a gradual and growing sense of being a failure throughout the many years of an individual's formal education. After all, as is discussed in Chapter 5, many people from all kinds of backgrounds and contexts fail in 'one-off' situations, including clever and prosperous students who 'flunk' exams. These failures for disadvantaged children may be the culmination of several years of what Reay (2017: 77) calls 'routine everyday humiliation and slights. In hierarchical systems of ranking, both of schools themselves and of learners within schools, poorer children are disproportionately found in the bottom sets or streams of secondary schools and there is a growing trend to setting and streaming in primary schools also (Reay, 2015; Smyth and Simmons, 2017). We are deeply influenced, especially as children, by the way we are seen and judged by others, and a permanent existence in the lowest groupings in the schools' systems inevitably brings a strong sense, not only of failure for the individual, but of collective failure (Parsons and Hallam, 2014). Research in recent years into well-being of children and young people across 20 countries (Hascher, 2011) found that children who are low achievers or perceived as low achievers had much lower levels of well-being than high achievers. Low well-being here related to self-confidence and personal belief in one's own abilities, and hopefulness for the future. In Green's (1992) study of education systems in three countries, it was seen that the working-class experience of education had overall been one of failure and not success and in no way perceived as one about offering opportunity to improve oneself. Those in the lowest sets or streams in many schools in this century appear to see themselves as having no opportunity to improve, as they see a placing at the bottom of a hierarchy as the indicator of their worth. There is clear evidence that children disadvantaged by social context are most likely to be in the most underperforming schools, and within those schools, may also get the highest proportion of inexperienced teachers, and the highest turnover of teachers (Reay, 2012; Reay, 2017).

A system of constant assessment in the school will regularly produce a rating for those children in the bottom groups of something seen as weak, or below standard, reinforcing the learners' self-perceptions. Such learners will be entered, if they are entered at all, for public examinations at the lowest level, with the higher levels reserved for higher sets. Even if a learner made rapid progress in a subject, it is not likely that they could be taken into the higher-level sets, because of the amount of work already covered in the syllabus or programme. Whilst good teaching may try to reward effort as much if not more than attainment, the experience of being permanently at the bottom can clearly drain the motivation for effort out of these children. The words of Stan, a senior teacher in a London borough secondary school serving a very impoverished area, perhaps sum up this dilemma. We interviewed Stan at the end of a school year when he was retiring after a lifetime career in teaching:

> I try hard not to be cynical, because I want to remember all the wonderful times I have had but – in recent years, and especially since we became an academy (which we resisted!) last year, I have been upset for our kids as they seem to have become less and less important to the powers that be – unless they are bright and toe the line. I have always liked the 'rebels', often bright boys or girls who would challenge you and make you think a bit more. Now they mustn't do that, and, you know, the middle-class kids know how to play the game – as their parents do. So they do okay. But the kids from poor homes – as soon as they step out of line, they are 'for it'! And what I see is bright kids in bottom groups put there because of misbehaviour and then they live up – or rather down – to what's expected of them and it's all downhill for them from then on. I break my heart when I see bright kids saying there's no point in trying. They say, 'We're told we are rubbish!' I can see them leaving school and telling their own kids what a rotten place school is – and surely that's a tragedy.

The consequences of the attitudes described in this section are explored later in Chapter 5.

Conclusion

In examining the way in which poverty and linked disadvantages affect children from impoverished homes, this chapter has:

- tried to indicate the way in which such children's daily lives influence their attitudes and outlook
- described how their natural talents and abilities may go unfulfilled because of being deprived of opportunities available to others – and
- shown how a growing sense of being a failure during and at the end of their schooling becomes almost inevitable

Chapter 4
The Implications of Underachievement in School

Introduction

In the previous chapter we looked at a number of case examples of underachievement of students in schools and colleges and the factors contributing to the problems they faced. In this chapter we will develop some of those issues and consider the consequences of relative underachievement in relation to education and to the wider society. We are primarily concerned with schools and colleges, but the issues arising from the educational gap are not solely confined to the education sector and they will impact on wider society. Schools and colleges will also connect with their local community in a variety of ways which are not always restricted to educational issues. In particular this chapter will:

- investigate the problems of underachievement in schools and colleges
- consider the impact of underachievement on school leaders and teachers
- highlight the problems faced by young people as a result of underachievement
- discuss the wider implications for society of underachievement in education
- put forward broader proposals about strategies to break the cycle of deprivation

The Problems of Underachievement in Schools and College

Organisations such as the Office for Standards in Education (Ofsted) 'make sure that institutions providing education, training and care services in England do so to a high standard for children and students' (Ofsted, 2020). They have 'high expectations for every child regardless of background. Everything they we do as an organisation is in the interests of children and students, first and foremost' (Ofsted, 2017). In England, the Ofsted judgement following a school or college inspection is likely to influence the choice of school for those parents or guardians who have the expertise and the resources to access that information. Parents will look to place their child in what they perceive to be the best possible school. However, for some parents there is often not a choice about which school to send their child. This can be due to a combination of factors including income, geographical mobility, childcare pressures, family, health and in some cases a lack of motivation. For more affluent parents it will be easier, for example, to transport their child to a school that is perceived to be 'better', than it is for poorer parents who do not have their own transport or who suffer from poor health. In some cases some parents will move to areas that have 'good schools', and this will drive up property prices – the so-called postcode effect. This prices out poorer families from the area and further reinforces the more affluent intake of local schools.

A bunching effect occurs, meaning that some schools have large intakes from what would be classified as poor backgrounds with all the problems that we have discussed in previous chapters. Of course many schools with an intake predominantly from less affluent backgrounds will do an excellent job and be outstanding schools. However, this situation creates added pressure for schools, and they have to deal with a range of issues unlikely to be faced in schools that recruit children from more affluent backgrounds. An example from a primary school we visited and an interview with a member of staff in the north-west of England illustrates one particular problem unlikely to be faced in more affluent areas.

Case Example 4.1

'I'm the member of staff in charge of coordinating our food policy. Funny really, I never expected to work as a primary school teacher and to be doing what I do. We have a real problem with hunger, that's right kids not having enough to eat. No child in the twenty-first century should be hungry. The emphasis in many schools is on their kids eating the right sort of food to tackle obesity. We have that problem but for many households locally they just don't have the money to give their kids enough to eat. So we've provided breakfast, toast and cereals, and of course many of them get free school meals. In the last six months we've gone beyond that and have started distributing food parcels to families. We're working with the local food bank and the supermarkets, who've been very generous as well as putting in food collection boxes, to ensure that families get the basics to supplement what they buy. I've started dreaming about packs of pasta and tins of beans! For some families we take it to them, if the parent is disabled and struggles to get out, for example, others we hand it out at school. It's been a real community effort and it has helped me to get to know some of the parents better and to have a real understanding of the circumstances some of them live in. Seeing the conditions in which some of our children live has been a real eye opener. We're now thinking of running cooking classes and doing things on healthy eating, but the priority for us really is about making sure our kids are not hungry when they come to school. Once you start this it's difficult to stop, parents come to depend on it, so we continue in the school holidays, volunteers help us to distribute food all year round.'

This account was from a successful school, which was doing well in raising the attainment levels of children from deprived backgrounds and perhaps it is an extreme example of how a school can become involved in an issue which some observers would see as outside their remit. However, it serves as an example of the wider implications of the education gap and how education is only part of a complex picture. Schools and colleges can find themselves working with a range of individuals and institutions to try and deal with what are often complex family situations. This can involve social services, the police and a range of health professionals. All schools will have their share of social problems to deal with, but these are likely to be increased in areas of acute deprivation with the subsequent impact on staffing and resources. Hutchinson, Reader and Akhal (2020) have estimated that children with a high level of poverty (those on free school meals for over 80 per cent of their time at school) have a learning gap of 22.7 months. They go on to claim that the proportion of pupils with a high persistence of poverty has risen from 34.8 per cent to 36.7 per cent which contributes to the failure to reduce the size of the education gap. The impact of child poverty on the ability of children to do well at school is a significant factor in ensuring the education gap has not been eradicated. While schools do their best to mitigate some of the issues, more fundamental changes in wider society are necessary. Improved health care, higher incomes for the poorest members of society, better housing and greater access to family support would all help to improve the life chances of the most disadvantaged members of society. These are outside the control or influence of schools and it is important to remember that schools operate within the social and economic norms of society.

Impact on School Leaders and Teachers

In the previous section we outlined an example of a school operating in a deprived area and the impact it had on the how they interact with their parents and community. We will return to this issue in more detail in Chapter 11. The focus of this book is what schools, their leaders and teachers can do to close the education gap and to improve the life chances of young people. A great deal of the literature rightly focuses on what schools can do, see for example Sobel (2018). However, at this stage we need to take a little time to consider the impact for school leaders and teachers of working in schools situated in areas with high levels of deprivation. As we have already identified, there are a range of potential issues to deal with that might not be faced in schools in more affluent areas. That is not to say that those schools in more affluent areas do not face problems, but the magnitude of the problem is likely to be different and greater in schools in more deprived areas.

There has been a great deal of literature on the importance of the head teacher and senior leadership in schools which raise attainment, and we will return to this in detail in Chapter 7. There have also been a number of accounts of their work by individual school leaders, for example Parker and Middlewood (2013). Middlewood and Abbott (2018) set out the key functions of leadership in schools:

> It seems to us that school leaders, by the very nature of being in the work of education of young people and children, will have a clear moral purpose underpinning both the vision for the school that enables it to have a sense of direction, and the strategies that are developed to enable that vision to be achieved. This moral purpose will similarly influence the way schools operate on a daily basis, and the values inherent in this purpose, therefore, frame the culture that pervades the school *(Middlewood and Abbott, 2018: 38)*.

In schools working in deprived areas with children from poorer backgrounds there is a desire to improve the life chances of young people. Generally schools are committed to try and compensate, as much as realistically possible, for the broader problems of society and of the home circumstances faced by some of their students. How does this impact in practice on the role of the head teacher in schools operating in deprived backgrounds? Case example 4:2 gives an indication of the added pressures faced by school leaders in such circumstances.

Case Example 4.2

Polly is the head teacher of a large secondary academy school in the south-west of England. It serves a deprived area. Many coastal areas in England have some of the largest educational disadvantaged gaps between students (Hutchinson et al., 2020). The school has experienced some turbulence with staff changes and a new senior leadership team. Student underachievement is a major problem and there has been a 'rebranding' of the school as part of an attempt to change the culture and the perception of the school from the perspective of parents and students. Polly explains some of the issues facing her as a head teacher:

'I wanted to change the culture and the way in which the school is seen and operates, high aspirations, no tolerance of failure. Some staff have had to go, but not enough really. When I came morale was very low and there was an acceptance of second best, it'll do. I wasn't having it, so we've made major changes. It's working, but the sheer scale of working in a school like this can be daunting. In any school there's often an issue in recruiting staff, especially in shortage subjects, but here it's much worse. I have to spend a great deal of time trying to persuade people this a great place to work and of course I want to keep my best people. Sometimes we end up with non-specialists teaching subjects, my head of modern foreign languages, for example, has taught some maths. She does have an A Level in it, but she's not a maths teacher. Then of course we have to deal with those staff who, to put it mildly, don't buy into the vision. They can undermine all the good work we've done. Managing resources, of which there are never enough is also extremely time consuming. Dealing with parents, outside agencies and so on could take up all my time, luckily, I've got a great team. Everything else that a head has to do, it's a battle sometimes to keep going, luckily, I'd worked in similar schools, so I knew what to expect. I know all heads have it tough, but some of them should come and try it here for a term.'

Changing and setting the culture of the school is often a major priority for head teachers and senior leadership teams in schools in deprived areas. A can-do and purposeful attitude and a lack of acceptance of previous perceived low standards is fundamental to their approach. This does create added pressure on the leadership team to ensure they achieve the high standards they are setting. No school leader or teacher sets out to fail and to run or work in a school that is not successful. We have to be careful to avoid using stereotypes and it is easy to categorise a school as failing without looking at the context. Many schools are doing a good job in difficult circumstances and it is worth remembering that there are many schools in affluent areas who are not necessarily doing their best. However, the impact on senior leaders of schools operating in deprived areas will be considerable.

Individual teachers will also face additional pressures working in a school which is situated in a more deprived area. Teachers may find there is greater student absence, increased poor behaviour, a lack of socialisation, a failure to engage and a lack of motivation. These issues can manifest themselves in increased pressure in the classroom and there are some teaching staff who will claim they are more like 'social workers than teachers'. The school have a responsibility to ensure policies are in place to minimise these issues and to support staff and students but there will inevitably be differences at classroom level. Some teachers are skilled at working with high achieving and motivated students, but find it more difficult to relate to those who are less committed. Ultimately this is a decision for individual teachers to make, but working in a school like the one described in the two case examples in this chapter can bring added pressures into the classroom. It may also bring additional job satisfaction. An important aspect of dealing with these pressures is appropriate staff development and support from senior leadership and we will return to this issue in Chapter 7.

One final consideration of the impact on school leaders and teachers is the effect of the COVID-19 pandemic and its impact on school and college students. As we pointed out in Chapter 1 the pandemic is likely to increase the size of the educational gap, as large numbers of students have missed a significant amount of time in school with a disproportionate impact on students in more deprived areas. All senior leaders and teachers in schools and colleges have had to respond to the changing situation as new regulations and restrictions have been put in place. Ranging from the placement of hand sanitisers, through year-group 'bubbles, to dealing with anxious parents and the wearing of face masks, all schools have had to deal with a range of additional pressures. For those who work in more deprived areas there are additional problems that put extra pressure on staff. We have spoken remotely to two teachers in very different schools to illustrate the additional concerns caused by the lockdown during the COVID-19 pandemic and the return to school:

Case Example 4.3

Wilf is Head of History in a fee-paying day school:

'We've had a lot of work to do putting material on line and to prepare for the return of students, lots of meetings on line. Things will be different when we return to school that's for sure. My groups have missed out but the engagement from parents and the students has been great. On-line learning was really well supported and if any kids went missing parents were quick to respond and get them back on track. If we didn't do what we had promised they also soon let us know. At school I also have students for a longer amount of time than I would in a state school so I'm feeling pretty confident we can catch up with anything we need when we go back. We know when they return to school there's bound to be issues, but we also know the parents will be informed and fully involved.

Annabelle is an assistant headteacher at a secondary academy in a deprived urban area with a large number of students who have English as a second language:

'It's been a tough time and we've got a lot of catching up to do. We've done a lot of planning to ensure we have a safe return to school, but I'm worried about the amount of time they've missed. We went on-line very early, there was good support from the school. But if I'm being honest a large number of our students didn't engage, on a good day we had 50 to 60% working on line. They tended to be the more able, for the less able it was much less than that. We've got a lot of work to do catching up. How will they re-engage with school work, will they see any point to it? There are some language problems with home. We were discussing what to do if we suspect a child might have the virus, we temperature-check everyone who comes into school. Do we send them home and get the parents to get them tested, we're not sure some will, or do we drive them ourselves to the test centre? On one level a small concern, but on another you can see the logistical and time concerns. It's going to be an even more interesting new term in September!'

The snapshots provided by Wilf and Annabelle in Case example 4.3 illustrate the different pressures affecting schools as a consequence of the COVID-19 pandemic. All head teachers and teachers have found their workloads increased as a result of the pandemic. For those working in more deprived areas with a larger education gap, the increase in workload is likely to be greater than their colleagues in schools in less deprived areas. A study into schools' responses to COVID-19 has reported that 'teachers in the most deprived schools are over three times more likely to report that their pupils are four months or more behind in their curriculum-related learning in July, compared to teachers in the least deprived schools (53 per cent compared to 15 per cent)' (Sharp, Nelson, Lucas, Julius, McCrone and Sims, 2020: 4).

The Wider Implications for Society of Education Underachievement

We have described and discussed the implications for individuals of a failure to achieve their potential and to have a full range of choices with the subsequent impact on social mobility in Chapter 1. For an individual student underachievement at school is likely to result in limited options in terms of employment and access to further education and training. This may well lead to a lifetime of reduced income and associated problems relating to health, housing and well-being. A full account of the consequences of underachievement at school for disadvantaged learners will be provided in the next chapter. However, these individual outcomes will collectively have an impact on wider society and the community as a whole. There is a moral argument that in any society the government has a responsibility to help to improve the life chances of the most disadvantaged members of society. There are different ways to achieve that aim, which we briefly considered in Chapter 1. In the United States, for example, President Trump believed it was best achieved through the market and subsequent job creation. His successor, President Biden, has adopted a much more interventionist approach, with a massive federal stimulus package to offset some of the potential inequalities of the market. It is not within the remit of this book to go into these arguments in any great detail, but policy choices have to be made by politicians. The failure to ensure that young people entering the labour market have been given the opportunity to make the most of their education and skills is likely to have a negative impact on the economy and on those individuals in terms of income and job opportunities. According to the Organisation for Economic Co-operation and Development (OECD):

> As countries struggle to respond to economic, environmental and social transformations – including technological advance, climate change and migration – intellectual capital has become the most valuable asset of our time . . . The demand for higher-order skills is both economic and social. The employment rate of adults with a tertiary degree is about 9 percentage points higher than those for upper secondary education only, and they earn on average 57 per cent more (OECD, 2019: 9).

A failure to ensure that the workforce of a country is able to be as productive as possible can have a serious impact on economic performance and prosperity. The Institute for Fiscal Studies (IFS) has estimated that 'one factor driving higher productivity in London is the fact that it has a more highly educated workforce than other parts of the country' (Zaranko, 2020: 1). A highly skilled workforce is essential if a country is going to be economically successful and have good rates of economic growth. A sizeable education gap will not lead to a positive economic outcome, as a significant amount of human capital will not be utilised to its full potential. In strict economic terms, it is advantageous for a country to ensure that the highest possible proportion of its population have high levels of education.

In countries which have high levels of income inequality, such as Italy, the United Kingdom and the United States there is less social mobility across generations. Countries which have a more equal distribution of income, such as the Scandinavian countries are likely to see higher levels of social mobility (OECD, 2018). The increased ability of better-off parents in countries such as the United Kingdom and the United States to invest in education, given the disparity in incomes, will only tend to make the problem worse and make it more difficult to reduce the education gap. As a consequence, a range of organisations (e.g. government and charities), will attempt to mitigate this effect through targeted policies. We looked at the work of some of these organisations in Chapter 1. In some countries, such as Norway and Sweden, there is a different approach with much more emphasis on reducing income inequalities through progressive taxation and government expenditure.

Wide differences in income between different groups in society can also lead to a range of social problems. For example there are likely to be higher crime rates per head of population if people consider that they do not have a stake in society, and they have nothing to lose. Physical and mental health problems are likely to be greater, which again will contribute to poverty and greater inequality. Poor housing and a damaged environment will make these issues worse. There is a danger that there is negative reinforcement of the education gap, which is passed on from one generation to another. The next generation see the hopelessness of the older generation and have little incentive to invest in their own education and training. Some areas become associated with low levels of educational attainment, increased poverty and crime. Schools and colleges will have a role in breaking this cycle, but they cannot work in isolation and there is a need for more wide-ranging policies to alleviate the problems.

Strategies to Break the Cycle of Deprivation

In Chapter 11 we will put forward some suggestions for specific education policies directed at reducing the attainment gap. At this stage we will briefly suggest some more general policies that the state could implement to reduce some of the causes of deprivation. An obvious response would be to increase the income of the poorest members of society, through redistribution of income though taxation or increasing state benefits and other payments that are made to the poorest members of society. In effect, there would be a major redistribution of wealth from the richest to the poorest members of society. This is a feature of countries such as Sweden, but not, for example, the United States. Such a redistribution of income would increase the amount of income poorer members of society have to spend and could lead to an improvement in areas such as the general health of the population and the quality of housing. Additional resources from the higher taxes paid by the wealthier members of society could be used to fund additional expenditure on education and training benefiting those schools and colleges that work with the most disadvantaged students. This would achieve a fairer distribution of resources and create a more equitable society. However, there is no guarantee that this redistribution would necessarily lead to an improvement in students' attainment levels at school.

Those opposed to a major redistribution of income would argue that it is necessary to allow individuals the choice to improve their life chances through their own efforts and hard work. Having winners and losers is a fact of life and young people need to get used to this as they go through life. In a competitive environment, rewarding hard work and individual aspiration is seen as the best way to improve the well-being and wealth of society. Supporters of this approach would argue that a major redistribution of income through taxation and government spending would penalise those members of society who have worked hard and improved their income and prospects. In effect, this redistribution of income would have the opposite effect and lead to people being less prepared to work hard and to take risks because it would be taken from them in higher taxes, and there would be little incentive for individuals to work or invest to improve their life chances.

We are not in a position in this book to consider these differing approaches in detail, or to favour one over the other but they are worthy of further thought and discussion. However, what the state can do is to try to create a more level playing field through ensuring that there are opportunities for all, and that basic infrastructure is in place to support attempts to close the gap. An example of this is the current UK government's so-called 'levelling up agenda'. Although currently light on any specific detail this policy is designed to provide greater opportunities for people who live in deprived areas and to redirect resources from the more prosperous areas of the country to the poorest. In part this is a political initiative designed to maintain voter support in those areas, but many of the areas have been starved of significant investment and seen traditional industries decline with a major loss of employment opportunities especially for the poorest members of society. In the United Kingdom, investment spending, for example, is higher in London than other parts of the country, £1,456 per head compared to an average of £891 per head in the rest of the country (Zaranko, 2020). Another aspect of this policy could be to transfer public sector jobs from London and the south-east to other parts of the United Kingdom. The intention behind these policies is to provide more employment opportunities for the more deprived regions and to increase income levels leading to a levelling up between the disadvantaged and more prosperous areas of the United Kingdom. This could lead to an improvement in the educational performance of the students from the poorest backgrounds. In England, the areas with the lowest GCSE disadvantage gaps, are found in London, whilst the highest are in areas of high deprivation in the north and in a number of coastal towns. The GCSE disadvantage gap is the difference between poorer students and their peers in terms of how far they are behind in years when they take their GCSE examinations. For example poorer students in Blackpool, a coastal town in north-west England, were found to be 26.3 months behind their peers by the time they reach their GCSE examinations at the age of 16 compared to 0.5 months in Westminster in London (Hutchinson, Reader and Akhal, 2020). We do have to be careful using these figures, because although Blackpool is generally a much poorer area than Westminster, there will be significant differences in income within areas such as Westminster. However, it does suggest that the policies that are being implemented in Westminster are generally having an impact in reducing the gap.

Across the world, governments are putting forward a range of policies designed to 'ensure inclusive and equitable quality education and promote lifelong learning opportunities for all' (UNESCO, 2015: 29). Different countries will adopt different approaches to achieve this aim. The underlying approach will differ between countries, with some favouring a more market and competitive approach to creating favourable conditions to reduce the gap and others taking a more interventionist approach in an attempt to bring about greater fairness and redistribution of income within the system. These society-wide general approaches to reducing the gap between rich and poor will underpin the specific approaches schools and colleges implement which we will discuss in more detail later in this book. However, it is important to bear in mind the underlying economic and social systems in which schools and colleges have to operate, whilst trying to do the best for every student. Schools and colleges have no control over this, and they are often placed in a situation where they have to attempt to mitigate the consequences of broader social and economic policies.

Conclusion

There are widespread implications for individuals, schools and their staff and for the wider economy and society from the failure to close the education gap. Government policies and the actions taken by schools can all have an impact on closing the gap. However these have to be supported by individuals and groups. Unless there is a greater interest in education and the opportunities that it can provide, it will be difficult to bring about the scale of change that is required. There has to be support for particular groups, and as we will see in the next chapter special attention has to be given to the role of the family. Without more involvement and commitment to education from families it is difficult to see how the situation can be improved systemically. There has to be greater investment in education and support for schools from parents and carers, otherwise policies that are put in place will struggle to deliver successful outcomes for young people. It is important to get the overall structures in place and to ensure that there is a system that enables change to take place but there has to be a corresponding level of support from individual parents and carers and young people to enable policies to be successful.

In this chapter we have:

- investigated the problem of underachievement in schools and colleges
- considered the impact of underachievement on school leaders and teachers
- highlighted the problems faced by young people as a result of underachievement
- discussed the wider implications for society and the economy of educational underachievement
- put forward broad proposals related to strategies to break the cycle of deprivation

Chapter 5
The Consequences of Underachievement in School

Introduction

In this final chapter of Part One, we consider the consequences and implications for those people who have underachieved at school because of their circumstances of deprivation, and the disadvantages they suffer as a result. The chapter therefore:

- notes how underachievement at school can lead to under fulfilment in many aspects of adult life
- reflects on how a sense of failure may impact on post-school life for these people
- considers how certain attitudes such as learned passivity, and indifference to education may affect their outlook
- describes and discusses related mental health issues
- discusses implications for further and higher education for those from disadvantaged contexts
- debates the extent to which the generational cycle of impact of disadvantage on schooling is inevitable

Some Likely Outcomes of Underachievement at School

There is clear evidence that underachievement at school, especially for those from poorer homes and disadvantaged households, is likely to cause various disadvantages in adult life. Those in this position are more likely to:

- earn below the average earnings of most members of society
- be unemployed for longer periods during their working lives
- receive social benefits
- have babies that are below average birth weight
- be in single-parent families
- have poorer health overall in their lifetime
- be involved in drug use
- be involved in petty crime
- become carers at home for another family member
- have a lower life expectancy than average

This is a forbidding list, and fortunately there are many exceptions to these depressing trends. But it is inescapable that tracing the life histories of people in adult life with some or most of the above as features of their way of life, will show that the majority of them can be found to have had a period of compulsory schooling which was one of low attainment, underachievement and generally not one of enjoyment. Just looking at the first point on the above list, we can note that in the pre-digital age, there was still mass employment available in a regional industry in most developed countries for educational low-achievers. Being employed for a reasonable wage meant you could be an accepted citizen and enjoy various relevant social and cultural activities. Now, almost certainly, in those same countries, only low paid, low-status jobs are likely to be available to school leavers with either no or poor exam results, in an era when many of those with university degrees and higher education diplomas are employed to do work well below what their qualifications could enable them to do.

The Sense of Failure

In Chapter 3, we noted that many young people reach the end of their statutory schooling with the feeling that they have not really succeeded in anything that mattered there. They therefore look back on their period at school as having been a failure. Many have achieved very weak or only mediocre results in their public examinations at the age of 16 and carry with them very limited prospects of obtaining reasonable employment because of low levels of qualifications. Many have had, at best, only modest records in such areas as attendance and punctuality, behaviour in accordance with school requirements, and membership of and participation in organised school activities.

However, this is less a matter of having 'failed' in particular tasks (e.g. in school or public examinations) than of carrying a sense of 'being a failure' as they progress through life and employment. This distinction is absolutely critical and is found in so many aspects of our research into how some schools and leaders have succeeded with disadvantaged children. This is worth reflecting on here.

Failing at a particular task is something that everyone experiences. It would be difficult to believe someone who claimed that they had never failed at anything, although there are exceptional people who seem to succeed at *almost* everything they try their hand at! After all, learning from failure is accepted as one of the most powerful and effective ways of learning (Honey, 1993). This is when someone takes the view that 'I will understand why that didn't work and next time I'll do it differently'. In fact, writers on learning organisations (such as Honey, 1993) suggest that this attitude is a key feature of successful organisations which continuously develop because they never stand still, but are always learning from experience including from errors.

However, this is completely different from someone feeling that they are a failure. Such an outlook may mean someone goes into a venture or undertakes a task with the feeling that it is most likely that they will not succeed, or the venture will fail. It can therefore spread to a broader outlook which involves an expectation that things will go wrong because they nearly always do.

'Nothing I do goes right.'

'This is bound not to work.'

'I seem to be useless at everything.'

From the positions reflected by these expressions, it is an easy step to:

'I don't know why I even bother to try'

'It's not worth doing anything because it won't work for me.'

For some adults, this surrender to any difficulty can become a way of life, and it is a small step to letting things happen, leading to some or many of the things listed at the beginning of this chapter's first section, such as petty crime, drug involvement and accepting the most menial possible employment. It is also likely to affect an ability to form stable or at least mutually rewarding relationships.

For others, the sense of failure can lead instead to a very aggressive attitude to take into adult life, reflected by comments such as:

'They are all against me and I'll get them back.'

'Someone's to blame for the mess I'm in, so I'll fight back.'

'They're no better than me and I'll bring them down.'

For these adults, the temptation is to become aggressive even where there is no need to be and this can equally lead to some of the problems mentioned and, as with the passive failures, difficulties in establishing stable relationships.

The differences between those two possible extreme approaches might perhaps be summarised as 'Questioning nothing or questioning everything'.

Attitudes Arising from School Underachievement

Learned Passivity

Carrying issues into adult life from having done poorly at school may, in some cases, make people develop a kind of shell, embodied in a character which needs assurance and, as noted above, will either seek to dominate others by aggression, or be very acquiescent and allow things to happen. Seligman's (1979) theory of learned helplessness is described thus by Parrish (2010: 123):

> For children who have come to perceive themselves as being incapable of succeeding at school, the expectation of failure, regardless of effort or practice, can prove a powerful disincentive, sometimes amounting to a self-fulfilling prophecy.

She points out that people who have come to perceive themselves as destined to be a particular type – in this case, not good at much – will have low expectations at the start of any new activity or indeed relationship, and this is likely to become self-fulfilling prophecy.

In terms of adult life possibilities therefore, a strong sense of failure at school can contribute to poor prospects in satisfying employment and home or household development. Furthermore, such passivity is likely to permeate all aspects of life, so that such people are unlikely to vote in elections, for example, to try to change things. At home, the lack of intellectual stimulation for the children concerned in the deprived homes can have a poor effect on their development (Parrish, 2010), placing them at a further and future disadvantage compared with children from more prosperous households in the next generation.

Two example of passivity have already been noted earlier in this book. You may recall that Emma, primary academy head teacher in a predominantly white working-class area, referred to many of her school's parents as being very passive. She also noted those parents' poor experiences in their own schooling. The second example was in the rural villages of a poor region of South Africa where the standard of education and the achievement of pupils was low, but there were very few signs of unrest. Is this because the people there accepted their situation as normal and had little expectation of any alternative?

Of course, as already noted, there are numerous exceptions to failure at school leading to failure in adult life, and two case examples here help to illustrate both the problem and perhaps a response.

Case Example 5.1

Brian, head teacher of a large primary school in an industrial city in the English North Midlands told us the following:

'We were having huge problems with a nine-year-old boy who was rude and disruptive and when he assaulted another pupil, without any justification, I had to act. When I received no response to my letters, I decided to visit the home. (The boy had been temporarily suspended from attending school.)

I was greeted by astonishment, then resentment, but finally, we had a lengthy talk which went much wider than the son's behaviour. The father told me he had hated school because he had constantly been told he was "thick". He had clearly carried that resentment all his life (he is early 40s now) and said he didn't see the point of it except for "clever clogs" people. He had therefore made clear to his children that if anyone (teacher or pupil) at school "tried to put one over on you", they should hit back, literally where necessary. I like to think our chat had a little influence, but I cannot be certain of course. We came to an agreement over one aspect of his son's behaviour at school however. When he told me he might "belt" (hit) his son if he misbehaved at home, I got him to agree that he could not do this at school. How? Well, I told him that as he was the "boss" at home, so I was the boss at school and as what he said went at home, so what I said applied at school. I would not tell him how to run his household and he should respect my way of running the place of work. He accepted this logic perfectly well and promised his son would not commit such an offence again (and he has not!) I am not happy altogether, but the values of home and school are so far apart that I have to consider it a small victory. As I reflected, it was clear that his own resentment of and attitude to schooling, based on his own experience, was at the bottom of it all and I can only hope that when his son is a parent, that a little of what we agreed has affected him as a parent in how he feels about school.'

Case Example 5.2

In this case, M------ came from a partially deprived home in terms of finance, one she describes as an ordinary working-class home and with the father mostly in employment. However, the father left the home when she was in her teens, although he continued to support the household financially, and things were emotionally unstable.

M------ is now in her late 30s and runs a successful beauty and hairdressing business. In an interview, she says,

'At secondary school, I quickly became labelled as not very bright by the teachers and therefore I was convinced I was pretty stupid! I was probably inattentive in classes and I know some of my teenage behaviour was awful, both in and out of school! I couldn't wait to leave school – didn't get much in the way of exams and, having always been interested in appearance, got a place on the hairdressing course at the local FE college. I found I was good at that and I liked it and things have gone well for me there. However, I would always avoid if possible, talking with clients who I thought were 'clever', in case I showed my pathetic ignorance of everything except hair and beauty! They might use words I didn't understand, for example! Eventually, I knew I had to learn something about business if I wanted my own one day, so I enrolled, in my mid-20s, on an evening course in business studies. To my surprise, I found I was quite good at this and wrote some reasonable pieces of work. I met other students, who'd done better than me at school but also wanted to do this, and my confidence grew. I began to talk to clients of any sort now and that included teachers, university lecturers, even authors! In their different ways, they made me realise that I *was* clever – if that is the right word – just in a different way from them. I also started reading novels and watching different things on television. It is important to me to help my son at school keep his confidence about his own ability, and not worry if he doesn't come top as long as he tries his best. Looking back, I see that some of my behaviour in my teens and early adulthood was because I felt that people saw me as a failure and I wanted to show them, not that they were wrong but that I didn't care!'

Thus the nature of failure in learning at school is significant, and the way it is managed by staff is extremely important and is discussed in the Part Two of the book.

Attitude to Education

Whilst there are some individuals who will admit that they did not do very well at school because of their own failings, such as bad behaviour or inattention, many others who did poorly carry negative attitudes towards schools and education in general into adult life. It is worth considering some of these attitudes, so that in looking at how change may occur, some foundations may perhaps be laid for the next generation of parents. In all the points below, we have used paraphrases which are adapted from actual words used by parents, either heard directly by the authors or quoted by school staff.

Resentment and Suspicion

If the best thing about your time at school was the day you left it (to roughly quote what some parents said to us!), then it is altogether unsurprising that you, as a parent, will feel a certain amount of resentment towards the school to which you are sending your child. After all:

- You did not ask to do this – you had to send them!
- You know what schools are like – you have been there!
- You expect there will be trouble ahead for you, as there was for your parents.

Thus, some parents especially those who live in deprived and neglected circumstances, begin with a suspicion about the school and a feeling that it will be adding to, and not alleviating, the problems that they already face. If we can recognise in our own lives when we have felt resentment, it is often about something at a distance, which we do not understand or empathise with, or which upsets the running of our lives at that point. With such an attitude of suspicion and resentment built in, many of those parents will find it difficult to view the school as a friend.

Most of all, as soon as the school asks them to try to change something about the child's behaviour, the parent will at once be alert to an implied suggestion that they are failing as a parent – just as they failed as a learner at school! In those cases, the cycle of perceived failure is on the road to being continued.

Hostility

In other cases, adults who were made to feel a failure at school – certainly as they perceived it – may adopt a much more aggressive attitude to school, because of the injustice that is seen to have been suffered. Perhaps a wish to assert to the 'enemy' that they were not the failure they feel they were viewed as being, makes them hostile to any representative of that foe. Thus hostile parents may have an inbuilt attitude which states, for example:

- If the school and the child fall out, you will always be on the side of your child, because you know how unfair schools can be.
- You are not going to have anyone, child, teacher or other parent, 'putting down' your child.
- If the school complains about your child or you in some way, it is bound to mean trouble of some sort and extra work! You do not want that!
- Anyway, if the school were a nicer place or better run, your child wouldn't need to misbehave or be inattentive!

Such parents form the group of regular 'complainers', ones likely to argue with school staff, ones who are clear that behaviour at home is not at all as described at school, and challenging any sanctions the school wishes to apply. They may even in some cases, actively discourage compliance from the child, although such cases are rare. The best schools and their leaders accept the need for any school to try to be constantly improving, and try to learn from every situation where things go wrong in links with parents.

Seeing the School as an Authority

For many families living in circumstances of deprivation, the school can be seen as one of a number of bureaucratic authorities which make their lives even more difficult than they are anyway. Sarah, a principal of a nursery school in a hugely deprived area of a town in the Scottish borders, put it this way:

> For those parents who have spent the first few years of children's lives struggling to provide for the family, applying for state benefits, sometimes in more extreme cases, dealing with violence and abuse at home, and being unable of course to pay for any child care, school seems to come at first as a relief-somewhere to send the youngster for a few hours a day! Then for some, there comes a shock – wow! They find they are expected to send or bring them in every single day and on time, then collect them – on time. What's more there seem to be all sorts of rules about what they can and cannot do! I think when they are asked to see the teacher or leader for the first time, it is like being summoned for being in trouble which some feel they have spent a lot of their life doing! Also, there are forms to fill in sometimes and this place is always asking you to do this or that! I hope I don't exaggerate but I am sure some parents, especially mothers here, do feel that way.

Sarah describes well how some parents feel about school in that, like all figures and institutions of authority, it is, as they see it:

- bureaucratic, demanding lots of paperwork, with lots of rules and regulations
- a surveillance body, watching you, and probably trying to catch you out doing something wrong
- ready to penalise you if you break their rules

- something to be outwitted or outfoxed if you can find a way
- something that can be unjust
- something that will ultimately always win if you take it on, because authorities always do

For families who are constantly dealing with authorities, such as the police, social services of various kinds, local councils and other governance bodies, the school may automatically be seen as another on the list. After all, they are 'told' to send their child to school!

Of course, many excellent schools and their leaders understand this and do first-class work in helping families to work effectively with them so that children and their parents all benefit. A school has the advantage over other authorities listed above in that it can provide an actual person to meet on a daily basis and so help to dispel the idea of some anonymous and faceless body which influences their daily lives without understanding. Some examples of this are shown in Part Two of the book.

Mental Health Issues

In the first two decades of the twenty-first century, the mental health of children and young people has been a cause of growing concern in several developed countries. Whilst conditions such as undue stress and depression have been an increasing problem among populations as a whole, the growth of the problem among children and young people has been significantly greater during this period. These two conditions – undue stress and depression – which affect mental health and well-being are perhaps the most common and are the ones we discuss here. They can, of course, be closely linked in many individuals. According to MPs on the House of Commons Health and Social Care Committee:

> Half of all mental health conditions occur by the age of fourteen. Around one in ten children are living with some form of diagnosable mental health condition. The poorest fifth of households are four times more likely to have a serious mental health difficulty as those in the wealthiest fifth (House of Commons Report, 2018)

Particular groups in disadvantaged contexts may experience specific issues leading to mental health problems, for example, refugee families including children seeking asylum. According to UNICEF (2018), many of the four and a half thousand unaccompanied asylum-seeking children in England in 2016 had experienced bullying at school, plus problems such as lack of concentration in class, absenteeism from school because of nightmares and insomnia, and self-harm and suicide attempts. All of these, the report states, could and probably would, have serious implications for their adult lives.

A certain amount of stress in human life is of course desirable, just as most if not all people have occasional short periods of being 'fed up'; it is when stress and/or depression persist over sustained periods that they can become disabling, so that the person concerned is unable to function normally. At times of extreme emotional stress, such as a family bereavement, if support is given, people often recover. Obviously, staff themselves within schools are subject to such stress and this needs to be managed (see Middlewood and Abbott, 2017, pp. 44–45). Case example 5.3 (below) shows how a problem at school developed into a severe mental health issue for both child and parent (and incidentally, the also teacher!)

Case Example 5.3

Through a local authority officer, we heard the story of Jason, a 12-year-old boy and his mother, Janice. It began with Jason arriving at secondary school incorrectly dressed – for the fourth time. The mother had not responded to letters sent from the school about this. Janice, the mother, later said she had not replied because she did not see why she should be humiliated by 'everyone' knowing she could not afford to buy the proper attire. The school later said that if they had known, they could have supplied the items for nothing or at very low cost. In the meantime however, Janice, a single parent, had gone to the local press, resulting in an article appearing in the newspaper, denouncing the school as 'unjust' and 'full of snobs'. The mother also appeared on local radio, claiming she was now 'on pills' and Jason was now uncontrollable at home. This is a concise account of a lengthy saga over several months, involving Jason missing school for that time. The officer who interviewed both parties felt that Janice had possibly instilled in her son a sense that he was being 'picked on'. Whatever the rights and wrongs of it all, and the officer stressed that the school was not known as an overly strict one and had good relations with most parents, Jason spent the rest of his compulsory schooling years in a Pupil Referral Unit (PRU), obtaining just one pass at his Sixteen Plus examinations. Janice remained on medication for a number of years and, at the time of speaking with the officer, was in dispute with a different secondary school about its treatment of her daughter.

We can note from this example, how a sense of unfairness triggered the whole situation, causing great stress to those concerned, and adversely affecting a child's schooling. It seems almost certain that Jason would carry a resentment of his treatment into the way he behaved as a parent himself.

As for depression, the following symptoms listed by Parrish, 2010, pp. 180–181) are a clear indication of how it can manifest itself at school, and will be recognisable to most teachers and school staff:

- irritability and diminished interest or pleasure in most daily activities
- oversleeping (often linked with insomnia at home)
- fatigue or loss of energy

- feelings of worthlessness and low self-esteem

- diminished ability to concentrate

- eating disorders such as anorexia and bulimia – evidenced in erratic dietary habits

(While some of these individually may apply more to male or female learners specifically, in general such symptoms are applicable to all.)

All these inevitably impact on any ability to achieve at school. Moreover, they are equally applicable to adult behaviour, and therefore may for some people be a continuous pattern

Most seriously, recurrent thoughts of death may occur, hence the worries about suicidal thoughts which concern so many educationalists and social workers. Modern issues affecting children's and adolescents' lifestyles, such as body image, self-harm and excessive use of social media, accentuate many of these issues and place greater pressures on adolescents' self-perceptions so that these are at risk of being carried into their adult life and into their own adult family households.

Implications for Continuing Education

Children from disadvantaged circumstances are much less likely to proceed to higher education institutions such as universities than those from more affluent homes. In the United Kingdom, the higher ranking universities have come under pressure from various governments in the twenty-first century to increase their intake from poorer backgrounds, as figures consistently show that the majority of students at Oxford and Cambridge in particular, have attended fee-paying schools. Between 2005 and 2016, the proportion of poorer students actually fell by over 2 per cent (HESA 2016). Furthermore, students from poorer backgrounds:

- tend to have a much higher drop-out rate (Vignoles and Powdthavee, 2009)

- tend to attend lower ranking universities (Reay, 2017)

- are more likely to take part-time jobs during their university period

- emerge from university with greater debt (Crawford et al., 2016)

- earn significantly less during their subsequent careers (Stevenson and Clegg, 2012)

Thus, even those from poorer households that do reach universities tend to have a much harder time, 'distracted by financial, health and family problems, and often lacking the confidence and self-esteem to be able to construct themselves as successful learners' (Reay, 2017, p. 125).

In some countries, such as England, there is also a regional aspect which can impact, so that the proportionate number of school leavers from the north-east of the country, one of the poorest regions, is significantly lower than those from the more affluent areas, such as the south.

Whilst we continue to stress that there are many exceptions to this and some disadvantaged families continue to encourage and support their children to try to continue education beyond school, for many it is clear that such education can seem rather pointless. There are also individuals who do go on to higher education, despite their family circumstances, but these are perhaps honourable exceptions to the general situation.

Similarly, in the United States, there is a general perception, according to Delisle and Cooper (2018), that the number of 'low income' students gaining entrance to elite colleges and universities has continued to decline in the twenty-first century, so that the Education Trust (2017) described some elite public universities as engines of inequality (p. 31). However, Delisle and Cooper's research (2018) suggested that the number of low-income students at elite or selective higher education institutions has remained stable since the beginning of the twenty-first century. They suggested that the situation for low-income students in terms of access and affordability was in fact 'less dire than many would have us believe' (p. 11). However, they found that the number of students from high income households had increased during the period 2000–16, and the decline was in fact from those described as middle-income households. In terms of 'narrowing the gap' therefore, such research perhaps indicates that, whilst things are not worsening for children from poor homes, they are not improving; and that children from affluent households continue to do best and the gap between these and all other groups has in fact widened.

Is the Cycle of Underachievement Inevitable?

In a book published in 2019, Vince explores the significance of social norms and their impact on societies and related cultures. The writer notes that social norms tend to classify particular groups as being at the bottom of a social hierarchy and these people do worse in everything from wealth to health. In one example, it is noted that certain minority groups in America – especially blacks, Hispanics and women – were more likely to be assigned irregular schedules of work and the harmful repercussions of this were felt not only by them, but also by their children in the next generation. The book argues that imposing social limitations on groups is grossly unfair and leads us to believe in our own successes being due to our own excellence and not to luck or social position. After all, this is much more convenient for us to believe, rather than the need to change society dramatically!

Meritocracy has been advocated as the way to overcome prejudice in favour of the privileged, of course. However, modern academics such as Markovits (2019) argue that meritocracy is in fact a sham. As globalisation and deregulation have made the business world more competitive and its jobs more financially rewarding, the premium on getting a high-class education and rising in a corporation has risen greatly. Focusing mainly on America and to some extent on Britain, Markovits shows that today the performance of American children born in 2000 was even more closely correlated with parental income than those born in 1950. Meritocracy, it is argued, has become the most effective way for the elite to entrench its privilege.

We can link this closely with the concept of social mobility which, in the view of Reay (2017), has an iconic status in English political discourse. Reay suggests that in England, the less mobility there seems to be, the more politicians propose policies to promote it. Some of the traditional ideas – and ones popular with conservative-leaning politicians – about helping disadvantaged people to achieve more, relate to social mobility – the notion that in the right society anyone is able to rise above their original status. One of two main ideas in England since the 1940s has focused on access to universities for children from poor backgrounds, discussed earlier. The second main idea has been that of selective schools, especially grammar schools, being available to those children.

Grammar schools were introduced through the 1944 Education Act and involved an examination at 11 years old to select more academically able children to attend these schools, which offered academic curricula. This system has polarised opinion between the conservative and socialist-leaning parties at least since the 1960s (see Chapter 1). For politicians on the right, grammar schools are an example of how children from working-class homes can 'escape' their backgrounds and aspire to cultural and material success. For others, grammar schools are an example of how many educational systems operate, so that 'winners and losers' are sorted in a way which prioritises and rewards upper- and middle-class qualities and, significantly, resources. Research from 2017, when the expansion of grammar schools in England was being enthusiastically advocated by the then prime minister, showed that to have even a 50:50 chance of getting into a grammar school, a child would need to be in one of the wealthiest 10 per cent of England's families (Burgess et al., 2017). The evidence has been clear for a long time. Even in 1972, in a review which looked at the English and Welsh selective schemes over nearly 30 years, Halsey et al. (1980) concluded that the middle classes had three times the likelihood of getting into a selective school than the working classes. Moreover, Reay (2017: pp. 33–39) gives details of how working-class children who were actually in such schools tended to be downgraded and emerged with weaker qualifications than those from more affluent homes.

There are some, therefore, who believe that those in more deprived circumstances will be able to lift themselves out of these contexts if social and especially educational systems provide the opportunities for this to happen. As already noted, the research evidence suggests otherwise. Often, the language of the adherents to this belief make use of the term, 'underclass' (Murray, 1996), to refer to a stratum of society which is mostly dependent on social security benefits and is blamed by some for being a threat to stability through such activities as drug use, gang warfare and criminality. We believe the evidence suggests a far more complex situation in which the inadequacy of certain environments needs to be understood and addressed, rather than focusing on the personal failings of those concerned.

In the United States, Rury (2014) noted that, throughout its history, the country had been slow to recognise and address the link between education and social change, but an awareness of how socio-economic inequality and cultural diversity had increased, especially in the largest cities, was likely to be changing this. The seminal 'A Nation at Risk' (1983) and more recently, 'No Child Left Behind' (1990) both stressed the vital requirement to focus on *all* children's needs being addressed, and thereby offering a hope that an emphasis on tackling the resources gap between the richest and poorest and therefore ultimately the attainment gap would become critical to the nation's future well-being.

Unless some of the environmental inadequacies already described can be addressed, whatever the precise setting, then the cycle of deprivation and educational underachievement may remain inevitable. Whilst this book cannot address all the related social issues raised, it will draw attention in Part Two to how the educational environment *can* be altered so that there are many fewer underachievers, and whatever students' circumstances, they will be able to face life after compulsory schooling with improved attitudes and prospects. The long-term view here is, of course, essential. Only when those future parents and indeed grandparents are able to send their children to school with some confidence that they will succeed, will a sufficient change occur to break that cycle.

Conclusion

This chapter has tried to give some of the evidence that shows that children from disadvantaged households who underachieve at school, are likely, in their given circumstances, themselves to become adults who perpetuate that situation. As parents, they seem likely to have families which have negative attitudes towards school, and often society in general. In a number of cases, they will encounter the same difficulties that their own parents did and are increasingly at risk of being involved in, and even contributing to, antisocial activities. There is a danger therefore that a cycle of such deprivation, disadvantage and underachievement may be in motion. This chapter has:

- noted some of the ways in which underachievement at school may lead to problems for those people in adult life
- reflected on how feeling a sense of failure arising from school may have a lasting impact on adults in various ways
- described how attitudes such as a learned passivity and indifference to education can be carried through in adulthood
- considered a few of the mental health issues that may emerge from all this
- discussed the extent to which higher education opportunities exist or are denied to disadvantaged children
- debated whether this generational cycle of deprivation and underachievement is inevitable

Part Two

Addressing the Problem

Part Two of the book focuses on what our research has shown about the schools that are successful with disadvantaged learners. We start with the more general principles and practice, and then examine each of what seemed to be each of four key elements in their success.

Chapter 6
The Key Principles for Action

Introduction

All the successful schools we visited appeared to have certain things in common, regardless of each one's specific context. Whether in an urban, rural, or suburban setting, whether the disadvantage related to poverty or acute social problems, whether the intake was multi-ethnic or mono-ethnic, whether primary or secondary stage of education, whether co-educational or single-sex, these schools had all succeeded in raising the attainment and achievement of their learners, sometimes to a quite remarkable degree. We have tried to analyse carefully what we might call the ingredients in these schools' recipes for success. In this chapter, therefore, we:

- stress the individuality of each separate effective school
- present some of the practices that were common to all of them in becoming effective
- describe the recruitment and deployment of the relevant staff
- identify the four key elements which seem to be central to the success of these schools and which are to be explored in subsequent chapters
- offer one extended Case example where all these elements cohere to give a picture of a highly effective school

The Individuality of Each Context and School

Whilst it is fairly well established that effective school leadership is contextualised (Bush, 2019), our research highlighted just how specific this contextualisation could be. The leadership aspects of this are dealt with in the next chapter, but here we draw attention to the uniqueness of each individual school, even where their contexts may appear quite similar. This is, of course, what makes the transferability of practice which was effective in one school to another apparently similar school so difficult to achieve. This point was emphatically brought home to one of the school leaders we interviewed. Nick had successfully led a medium-sized primary school in a very deprived area of an industrial city in the north of England. The school which had been rated as 'in special measures' by the inspection service Ofsted prior to Nick's appointment, had progressed to being rated 'outstanding' by the time he decided to move. After six years, Nick had successfully applied for the principalship of a larger school on the other side of the same city, which was also an area of considerable deprivation. This school had been designated as 'requires improvement'. Undoubtedly, a main factor in his selection had been his success in his first school as leader. Particularly because the situation was local, there was clearly an expect-ation he could repeat his success. Case example 6.1 is his story.

Case Example 6.1

'Looking back, it is now easy to see the mistake I made – assuming what worked in one school would work in another, when they seemed so similar. Both areas seemed alike; both were deprived, both had similar antisocial problems, both had families and parents who were positively anti-school. But when my first initiative of a families' space in the school did not work, I was taken a little aback. It was not until one day, I was put in my place by a father, a large, muscular unemployed dad(!), who told me in no uncertain terms that "We (the people in area X) are not like those _____ (people in area Y). Who wants to be like them! They are _____" (unrepeatable of course!)

I hate to admit it but he was right! To cut a long story short, the whole history in this area of the city was of resentment towards a major employer who had a generation earlier preferred to place a manufacturing plant in the other part of the city instead of theirs. Whilst of course there were similarities between the two schools' areas in terms of families' deprivations and poverty and so on, there was a fierce community cohesion which I had not found in the previous place and this cohesion was based on local history. I had to throw out my plans and start again! My starting point was a meeting about "What we are proud of in _____" I presented myself as the learner – which I was – and a listener. From then on, I slowly made progress and it took me even longer here to succeed and win the confidence of the families. So far, I have been here seven years and I still have a way to go, but we were graded as "Good" at our last inspection!'

There are probably a number of school leaders who have been appointed to second posts on the strength of earlier success, because it made sense for those appointing to do so. However, if even two apparently similar areas within the same city can offer such an experience for a school leader so that he learns not to assume they need the same practices applied, it is not surprising that we can say that we believe every single school context needs to be seen as unique. The Chapter 7, on Leadership and management, specifically, refers to this issue.

Whilst schools in similar disadvantaged contexts will probably have certain features in common, such as poverty, poor housing, low-level crime and others described and discussed in the earlier chapters of this book, leaders and others should be cautious of generalisations in thinking of strategies and solutions. Some of the different factors that might be relevant and worth consideration may include:

History of the area How long has it been a deprived area? How did this come about? Was it once reasonably prosperous, but now rundown? If so, why did that happen? Was it because of a major employer moving out or being shut down? Was it because of an influx of extra inhabitants? Did these people arrive because of strategy, such as 'London overspill', or by immigration? Were there funding resources removed by national or regional governments? Is it a rural area where many residents have moved to urban areas? Are there tensions in the area now whose origins lie in any of these?

History of the school itself Was it built when the area was different from what it is now? Are its facilities outdated and do they reflect the neighbourhood? Are they brand new and do they stand out in contrast to the surroundings? How many principals has the school had? How have they seemed to reflect if at all the community and its possible preferences (gender, ethnicity, age and so on).

Local customs and traditions Bush and Middlewood (2013) identified traditions (including myths and legends!), and heroes as factors which can strongly influence a school's culture that may, for example, exist when a new leader takes over a school. We encountered several of these through the experiences of leader interviewees. These included:

- The primary head teacher who made the mistake of abolishing 'birthday assemblies' which had always been held every Friday since the school opened. He was forced to re-introduce them when the overall attendance figure dropped so alarmingly. The reason for this was that he eventually found that previous heads had used the assemblies as 'inducements' to families and pupils to attend for the whole week; parents were invited to attend and hear their children acknowledged as long as their attendance had been 'reasonable'. When the assemblies went, so did the children! Until the new leader could achieve ways of getting the families and children to attend for positive learning reasons (which took time and was eventually achieved), the assemblies had to stay!

- In a school in a fairly remote village in a more deprived South African province, the children had one day a month off school to help local farmers with farm labour in return for some produce given free to the school. One school leader was shocked on taking up her new post that a 'hero' of the school's past was a student who had become a nationally reviled figure as a corrupt criminal! Resisting the temptation to simply attack the hero worship and 'expose' the person, she chose to focus on his background and education, including when he attended the school, and invite students to identify the forces that had made him take the path that he had, eventually turning him into a figure which, while not now admired, could be sympathised with. He could also be held up as an example of someone not using his abilities wisely.

Such factors as these underline the uniqueness of each school, and possibly the lesson to learn from them is that it might be preferable to see any benefits that lie within the existing features and, at least initially, work with these rather than the opposite.

Practices Common to all Effective Schools

Whilst we have stressed the uniqueness of each individual school's context and how important it is for leaders and others to recognise this, and whilst we have identified what we see as the four major elements in their success, it should also be noted that there are certain practices that need to be there in every school striving to raise attainment of disadvantaged learners. Perhaps these may be considered as the minimum requirements in school practice for success in this area to be achieved. Research from various sources over a period of time makes it seem clear that the following should be carried out:

- Identification of disadvantaged learners' needs (Raffo et al., 2007), Abbott et al. (2013), Carpenter et al. (2013). Obvious as this may sound, all research has found that unless the teaching and learning is targeted at the specific needs of the learner, no increase in knowledge or understanding can be certain. Thus unless the identification of each learner's specific needs is made, little will be achieved. Effective schools did this and thus focused on teaching and learning so that each individual could feel that it applied to him or her specifically.

- Collection, updating and reviewing of data (Abbott et al., 2013), Carpenter et al. (2013), Dunford (2014). These schools were data-rich, held extensive information on every single learner and ensured the data was regularly added to, amended, updated. Past records were important, as well as the most recent ones. A significant proportion of these schools had a member of staff (often a senior one) who had overall responsibility for this task. Some schools were meticulous in the precision of their data, so that even a small deviation from what was expected could be immediately noticed and acted upon if necessary. This all had to be done in such a way that the data did not become more important than the actual individual person.

- Developing strategies for support and interventions (Abbott et al., 2013), Carpenter et al (2013). With the required data always available, the schools were able to make informed decisions on what action to take to remedy a weakness, to pressurise for improvement, or to ensure no slippage. After a while, they had well-established systems which could be operated in virtually all circumstances as needed for any learner or group of learners. Many interventions were on a one-to-one basis, and many others on a small group basis, depending on need. Examples included learners with no access to computers, learners with first language difficulties, learners with high abilities in specialist areas, learners with special needs, whether slight visual impairment for example, or dyslexia or others. By far, the commonest areas for giving additional support were those in literacy and numeracy. This last area was the one that needed the most attention and it was seen as critical that such support was given as early as possible.

- Regular monitoring and reviewing of progress made (Abbott et al., 2013), Carpenter et al. (2013), Dunford (2014). None of these schools ever remained static in their development, being insistent on constantly checking and monitoring individual progress. Some did this by regular specific days or dates, whilst others preferred random and frequent processes. In all cases, wherever evidence of any falling-off for any learner was evidenced, this was investigated by the designated person (normally a mentor of some kind) and action taken. Such action could include a respite, where the falling-off was seen to be due to a negative change in personal circumstances, such as a family tragedy.

- Getting feedback from learners (Abbott et al., 2013), Carpenter et al. (2013), Dunford (2014). In Chapter 11, we explore the issue of learner voice generally in effective schools. Here we note that they all tried to ensure that individual learners, whatever their circumstances, had the opportunity to give feedback on their own progress, how they perceived it, and to debate with a mentor the extent to which what they were doing was effective and the right thing for them. Adjustments and even a change of direction could be made in the light of this feedback.

- All these practices can be seen to be integral to establishing the groundwork culture within which leaders and staff can develop the key elements to achieve the highest possible standards for each individual learner. They are summarised in Figure 6.1 (Middlewood 2019, p. 303).

If we pause for a moment, a question that lies at the heart of the whole question of success in education may arise. That is, if everyone knows what the right practice is, why can it not be done everywhere?

The answer surely lies in the fact that education is a 'people business' and human beings are different and unpredictable! Although we know what should be done, it is the way it is done and how it is applied that makes the difference. Having the right people there to do it is crucial.

Figure 6.1 Factors in developing effective school practice for raising attainment of disadvantaged pupils

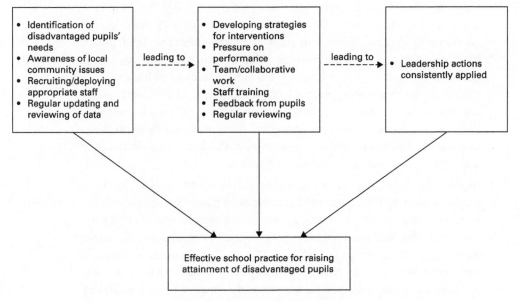

Recruiting and Deploying Relevant Staff

As Figure 6.1 suggests, having the right staff and using them in the most effective way for the benefit of learners is absolutely crucial to success, especially when working with learners who may have particular problems. By 'staff', we mean every person who is employed to work in the school. Teachers are central of course, but the roles of support staff such as teaching assistants (TAs), technicians, clerical and administrative staff are also vital. Certain key principles may be suggested:

- Increasing numbers of staff does not necessarily improve learning

  When the pupil premium funding for poorer pupils was introduced in England, many schools opted to spend the additional money on extra support staff, such as classroom teaching assistants. This did not prove successful.

- Commitment and attitude is critical

  We have previously referred to situations where certain teachers had to leave because they did not have what the leader was certain was the right attitude to or belief in what the children in that school could achieve. This is also shown in the Case example 6.2, and in nearly every school, interviewees stressed that belief in everyone's ability to achieve was the most important factor of all.

- The teachers have to be very good!

  This seems so obvious as almost to not need stating, but every piece of research into raising attainment refers to 'good teaching' as being central to achieving this. This professionalism was fundamental to raising attainment.

One indicator of a good teacher is the willingness to continue to learn as a reflective practitioner. Figure 6.1 shows staff training as a key element in success and is discussed in the next section as one of the four key elements, and later in Chapter 9.

Recruiting and Selecting Staff

As noted earlier, new leaders often found they had to 'move on' staff who were less competent or who did not have the right attitude. Also, in schools in deprived and disadvantaged areas, staff turnover is normally much higher than average, so early on in a new leader's tenure, there are likely to be opportunities to appoint new staff. Most of the interviewed leaders seemed to take an assertive approach to recruiting and selecting new staff in that they set out to offer the school as somewhere for new people to succeed and they said they tended to look for 'bright, enthusiastic, hard-working' people to join them in 'our enterprise here' (as one principal said she liked to describe it). One school in a London borough took potential staff members round the area in a minibus, so they could see the conditions in which many of their students lived. Frank, the principal, said there were usually three basic reactions:

'Some were appalled and decided against carrying on with their applications, so they de-selected themselves, which was fine. The second group were those who felt sorry for those who lived there; they were possibles for me, and it was something we could probe at an interview to see what they were prepared to do about it. The third group were those who basically said "Right, we've got to do something about this – that's what education is supposed to do". They usually got the jobs!'

When staff did leave for legitimate reasons, for promotion or family reasons, most leaders said they had learned the lessons of their previous experience that they should not look to replace like for like (see Bush and Middlewood (2013), chapter 9). As Susan, the principal of an academy in South Wales, expressed it, 'Even when it's one of your best people leaving, you have to see it as a chance to re-shape, to liven things up, and just keep remembering that no one, certainly not me, is irreplaceable. The children deserve the best and that's what you have to keep thinking of when you appoint anyone to a post.'

Using the Right Staff in the Right Place

Although new school leaders did sometimes 'get rid' of some staff they felt to be unsuitable, many also recounted how they had found teachers and other staff who were clearly perfectly capable but who in the words on one principal 'left battered and bruised by years of battling against the odds'. Another noted that 'They had survived by doing a great job for the few youngsters who wanted to succeed against the odds. This showed that they were in fact great teachers – it was a case of getting them to believe that if they could do that for a few, they were good enough to do it for the many, in fact for everyone.' In many cases, it was a question of getting the 'right peg in the right hole', as described by one head teacher. Some leaders had carried out skills audits on arrival, and moved staff to more appropriate roles; in some cases, this was simply a 'refresher' after years of doing the same work. Examples included a head of a large subject department becoming the school's special educational needs coordinator, a teacher in charge of music becoming a leader of 'learning to learn' initiatives in the school, and a teaching assistant becoming the lead learning mentor for a whole year group. In at least two cases, these changes involved a voluntary demotion where someone who had been a head of department and, grown tired of administrative duties, became a reinvigorated classroom teacher (in one of these the leader had managed to arrange a financial compensatory deal for the demoted person).

The Four Key Principles

Referring again to Figure 6.1, we can see that the elements in the boxes on the left and in the centre will not lead to success unless they are driven by, and are as a result of, leadership actions. School leadership is fundamental to its success in raising attainment levels and putting an end to underachievement in each of the schools researched. Whatever their context, and whatever stage they were at in the path to success, leadership was crucial. Whilst the principals and head teachers of these schools were very different in nature and personality, they had certain qualities in common. *School leadership and management*, therefore, is the first of the four principles we see as the key to having the opportunity to change the future for learners from disadvantaged contexts and the Chapter 7 is devoted to this subject. Whilst we have mentioned the individuals who held leadership posts, it does not mean in any way whatsoever that these schools were 'one-person' organisations. Nothing could be further from the truth: leadership permeated these schools at all levels and the following chapter describes and explains this.

The second of our four key principles is *collaboration*. Each of these schools had a commitment – often overtly stated but occasionally implicit – to everyone working together. Although a huge amount of work with disadvantaged and sometimes disaffected children and young people was done on an individual basis, we repeatedly found that these individuals wanted to stress that they never felt as if they were on their own. Communication networks were mostly invisible but highly active. Some schools did have formal written and/or graphically presented channels of communication for their employees, but these appeared relatively unimportant on a daily basis, and only tended to be used when an especially formal process was under way, such as a major disciplinary procedure. This collaborative approach operated at all levels, and is fully explored in Chapter 8.

As noted earlier, good professionals are always keen to learn and to adapt. The third of our key principles therefore is of *staff training and development*. All these schools had a strong commitment to staff training and development and many leaders linked this with recruitment and selection, in that they said no one could be appointed who did not have a commitment to their own future learning. Training was at all levels of staff, and tried to address individual, team and sometimes whole-school issues. Over half of the successful schools had an emphasis on in-school development, with needs identification through in-house inquiry. Chapter 9 deals with staff development in detail.

The final key principle is that of *community involvement*. Without exception, all schools had made huge efforts to involve families and parents in their plans and procedures for improving learners' attainment, recognising that the disadvantages that learners encountered began outside of school. The majority of these schools had gone beyond involving families and were trying to engage other community members in the school's work and life. Some had gone further than others, whilst a few felt their school improvement was part of what they saw as actual community transformation. This is all described fully in Chapter 10. Case example 6.2 shows all four principles at work. It deals with a school that suffered enormous socio-economic disadvantages, but which is now achieving good results and was graded as 'outstanding' at its last inspection in 2018.

Case Example 6.2

The school is in an extremely run-down and neglected area of London. In 2013, a television reporter for a documentary programme on city neglect described its high street as 'one of the most depressing sights possible. Over 60 per cent of the shopfronts are boarded up with the glass cracked or shattered. Graffiti covers virtually every wall and the litter is everywhere, whilst dog mess takes a good deal of avoiding! The smell is awful. A few businesses seem to operate, mostly betting shops and small convenience stores. Half of the street lights do not work, and I'm told most of these have been out of action for at least a year. An oddly incongruous Methodist chapel stands at one end of the street, whose walls also have some scrawl on. Just behind the high street is the local comprehensive school with a barricaded entrance and a worn sign saying " ――――School". Few people are in the street as we film, but one man, emerging from a betting shop, tells me that he went to that school as a teenager and it was "alright then, I suppose, but it's gone right downhill since those days. Most of the kids now don't bother – and I can't say I blame them."

The programme had also noted that, in the first decade of the twenty-first century, the area had been a stronghold of Britain's far-right party who had focused their anti-immigration policy on this neighbourhood and had had its headquarters in this street – it was now one of the boarded-up buildings.

Such was the picture given in 2013. When we visited the school in early 2018, our walk through the same street to reach the school took us past a bingo hall with flashing neon signs, a laundrette which appeared to be bustling, and several shops with goods displayed outside on the pavements. The amount of litter looked about the same as any average town or city, and likewise for the graffiti – and there were several 'poop scoop' points. Interviewing the principal, Wanda, who joined the school later in 2013, we drew her attention to the difference. Wanda's story:

'Oh, yes. I remember that documentary! I saw it ironically just after I accepted the job of principal here in May that year. A friend told me about it and told me I must be mad taking the job! It had been advertised three times and there had been very few applicants. Looking back, I probably was mad! But I thought two things. Firstly, no one expected too much of me here so what had I to lose?

Secondly, much more important, surely the children and young people deserved better than this! A kind of missionary zeal, I suppose. I said to myself that people shouldn't be living like this and if I can do a bit for the next generation of adults here, well, I'll be proud of that.

In July and September, I met all the staff – the majority of whom, unsurprisingly, were depressed and disheartened. Some were clearly thinking "She won't last long!" I had made a resolution that my biggest feature and asset or weapon would be my smile! When everyone's miserable, seeing a smile is a tonic, I believe. Several of the staff as well as the students clearly thought I was nuts! But I didn't mind that – there are much worse things after all. I walked around, smiling at people mostly, including any parents I met – and I didn't see many of those then,

I can tell you! My predecessor apparently had a reputation as a no-nonsense person apparently, so at least I was different!

Then we got down to it! Motto was "We *all* matter!" Every single staff member, every student, even those excluded at the time, every parent, every visitor. I came in at 7.30 each morning, left at 7 at night. Slept most of Friday night and Saturday though! We got rid of a few teachers but most wanted to stay. My favourite was a long-serving deputy who had five years to retirement. I offered him early release and to my surprise he said, "No. I thought I was leaving teaching fed up, but here's a chance to go out having done something." He was amazing. He retired last summer and we gave him a wonderful send-off! Lots of staff followed his example, including several brand new teachers. It just took off! We agree that if any staff member failed on something, as long as they'd tried, we'd back them. And over about two years, most were working as hard as could be, and the place was almost buzzing. Everyone had a mentor of some kind, every student, every staff member. No one was ever to feel alone. Most of our early training was in mentoring – much later we introduced peer mentoring for some students. I also had some Teach First young teachers in here and they make an impact and move on. Mind you, two of them insisted on staying after their three years and one is still here, a senior teacher now.

I had once on a teacher exchange, spent a term in a downtown New York community school a few years earlier and remembered that the school should be the natural centre, because everybody goes to school. We opened up the school for parents and families and got support staff to visit homes, child centres and anywhere where parents might be. Gradually they came into school and not just to complain! Then we had what we all need at some point – luck! The council invested a large sum of money in "community projects". This meant places opening up to be non-profit shops, workshops to repair and recycle all kinds of goods. Well, we had to be at the centre of that! We offered our spaces for evening and holiday workshops, for youth facilities, for sports groups, for a café for storytelling and music. I could go on! Lots of staff, students and families seem involved in various of these, and one or two of our most difficult parents originally are now actually running an activity. I think the gang culture that looked as if it was beginning to grow isn't now taking hold here and I don't think there is a significant drug problem – I hope I am not deceiving myself of course. As you can see outside, it's quite a vibrant place now and I love it! I give the credit to the whole neighbourhood people – they rolled their sleeves up and turned things round. Mind you, there's still a long way to go. And I'm going to be part of it!'

Those final words of Wanda's might seem an appropriate way to end this chapter. No matter how successful these schools had been in raising attainment for their learners, there never seemed any sense of complacency. There was always a sense of striving to do even better.

Summary

This chapter has:

- stressed that each individual school is unique
- described the various practices that are found in schools that are effective in raising the attainment of disadvantaged learners
- described the recruitment and deployment of school staff in these successful schools
- identified the four key elements that lie at the heart of the success of these school
- given an extended Case example of one such school which has these elements as the root of its success

Chapter 7
School Leadership and Management

Introduction

This chapter deals with the first of the four key principles shown by our research to underpin success in raising the attainment levels of disadvantaged children in schools, whatever the specific context – namely school leadership and management. It specifically:

- outlines some of the concepts of leadership which are relevant here
- stresses the importance of recognising leadership at various levels within the school
- examines leaders' relationships and communications with other staff, including the language used
- describes leaders' relationships with learners
- notes the qualities displayed by senior leaders and their emphasis on values in action

Which Model of Leadership?

Whilst the emphasis in the research and the conclusions drawn from it are essentially practical to enable leaders to learn from it all, it can be helpful to set these conclusions in the context of other research and literature on school leadership. There is a very extensive literature on school leadership and management which has developed since the 1970s and 1980s. This has enabled scholars to propose various models of educational leadership which appear to fit the practices and approaches which prove effective in leading schools successfully. (For a valuable summary of the majority of these models, see Bush (2019).) Our research suggests that what Harris and Jones (2019: 268), describing effective leadership of schools in challenging circumstances, called 'instructional leadership practices and transformational approaches', is very close to what we found displayed by school leaders in schools with large numbers of disadvantaged learners. In effect, this means that these leaders placed a huge, even relentless, emphasis on teaching and learning in their everyday practices and this strategy was part of their commitment to transforming their schools into places that fitted a vision shared with others, which embodied high expectations and high attainment.

However, there is another dimension to what the research showed as being fundamental to success in these contexts, and that is integrity. In leadership models, this is best described as 'moral leadership' and/or 'spiritual leadership'. The school leaders we encountered who had achieved success with disadvantaged learners showed such qualities as 'a profound sense of care' (Harris and Jones 2019: 265) and a 'strong commitment to equity and an inherent sense of moral purpose' (Fullan, 2007: 41). They also exhibited a clear understanding of the vulnerability of their pupils and a deep compassion for them – qualities referred to by writers on spiritual leadership such as West-Burnham (1997). West-Burnham suggested that moral leadership had two dimensions, one of which was some kind of spiritual power. In a faith school, this can clearly be related to the religious belief embodied in the school, but it is equally significant in many other schools. He describes the second dimension as moral confidence, meaning that leaders possess the ability to act in a way that is consistent with a clearly defined ethical value system.

Whilst a strong emphasis on instructional leadership has often been suggested as the key to leaders' raising attainment and turning low-achieving schools into high-achieving ones, we see the possible limitations of this as being the potential for a narrow focus that can develop in attempting to ensure that learners achieve success in measurable outcomes such as tests and examinations. Such success in raising measurable outcomes became notable in both the United Kingdom and the United States for example, but such leadership of 'turnaround schools', as they have become known, is now widely discredited. Its reliance on the apparent 'heroic' model of leadership of a single person who makes an immediate impact is seen as a weakness because the impact fades, sometimes very quickly, when that particular leader moves on. Such leadership can still be seen to be valued by both some governments seeking a quick rise in national attainment, and even perhaps within state schooling in some developed countries such as the United Kingdom, where a certain number of groups of schools (known as Multi-Academy Trusts – MATs) run by people from business backgrounds, also wish to achieve high ratings quickly in schools previously perceived as underachieving. This is entirely inadequate for schools in the context we are concerned with, because success in public examinations in schools in deprived contexts can sometimes be at the expense of the 'weakest' students (those likely to get low grades in these exams) who have been removed from school rolls. In England, it is estimated that some 7,700 of these 'lost' or 'invisible' children have been permanently excluded from schools (Timpson, 2019). It was also estimated that about 6,000 children were attending unregistered or illegal schools. At least half of these attended because of fears of not being accepted at 'proper' schools (Ofsted, 2019). This situation is not within the scope of this book, but it is worth noting because the schools we describe show that it is possible to succeed with *all* pupils regardless of background. Schools that can truly be described as successful are, of course, those that manage to get virtually every single person on the school roll to achieve their potential, whatever their circumstances.

Thus, school leadership in the contexts researched in this book seemed to be grounded in an approach which may be described as transformational, underpinned by a deeply moral and spiritual commitment to the learners in the leaders' care, who showed a deep understanding of the vulnerability and needs of these learners. To achieve the aims necessary, they placed great emphasis on learning and teaching – and our placing of learning before teaching is deliberate here!

Leadership at Various Levels

If leadership in schools is more about influence and not merely about authority, as suggested by Bush and Glover (2002), then in any organisation, the influence of people anywhere in it regardless of official position can be significant. In the most successful schools we researched, whilst the influence of the principal in developing the ethos of the whole school was huge, the more immediate impact on learners was from their teachers and assistants. This, of course, is fairly obvious as it is these people who have the immediate contact – mostly in class – on a daily basis. But in considering whether such people are showing leadership, it was clear that many of them did feel able to take individual decisions that they felt were in the best interests of specific learners – as long as these were in accordance with the values to which everyone was committed and on which the whole school ethos was built. The words of Jenny, a classroom teacher in a hugely deprived secondary school in a West Midlands conurbation in England, express this:

> We are all on a mission here – to help these young people overcome their incredible handicaps and we all feel the same about knowing they *can* and *will* succeed, so I don't have to go running to my HoD every time I want to do something special for one of my group. She knows I will have done it for the right reasons and, furthermore, if it goes wrong at all, it's my responsibility more than hers. Of course, I will keep her and others informed – that's in everybody's interest – but I have to stand by what I do. If it doesn't work, I don't need anyone else to remind me next time I might consider doing it – although they might remind me anyway! – I'm as aware of my failures as anyone. I'll endlessly discuss with colleagues what to do, but it's down to me.

We believe Jenny is describing and showing leadership here and there has been significant movement away from 'solo to shared' leadership (Crawford, 2012) in the twenty-first century. She attributes this partly to the disaffection with the heroic model of leadership, referred to earlier. Whether it is labelled 'shared', 'collective' or 'distributed' leadership (the normative term, according to Bush (2019: 10)), is less important than what actually happens. There is some debate as to whether distributed leadership is genuine leadership, or merely delegation, or an issue of power (Lumby, 2013). What seems to be crucial for such leadership to be effective at various levels within a school is that those in formal positions of authority, such as Jenny's HoD, do not feel threatened, or their authority undermined in any way by it. It is different therefore from delegated authority, although this is, of course, also present in any such school to enable it to run smoothly.

We found examples of initiative-taking like Jenny's in every school researched, with deputy head teachers, heads of faculties, classroom teachers and support staff all feeling empowered to act in good faith without constant reference back to someone in the chain of command. Gwen, a teaching assistant in a primary school, told us:

I was working on a one-to-one basis with Jason, a ten-year-old with weak literacy skills and a record of poor attendance. One day, in an outburst, he told me something quite shocking about his home and, having said it, told me if I ever told anyone else, he would never come to school again. I promised to say nothing but also offered to help him privately. Without giving any details at all, I told my principal of my undertaking who said, 'Well, you probably shouldn't have, but as you have promised, you must do whatever it is. Do it and don't tell me except when it has finished. Good luck.' It took a lot of my time and energy for the next year but somehow, Jason and I got through and when I last saw him, he told me he was doing 'Pretty good' at secondary school.

The willingness of senior leaders to enable staff at all levels to take ownership of a problem or situation and deal with it as they think appropriate is seen as a major factor in staff motivation and morale (Bush and Middlewood, 2013, Middlewood and Abbott, 2017). Certainly, staff in the schools visited seemed very confident about their ability to manage tricky situations and their confidence to be able to do so, with one all-important proviso of course – that the principal would back them if something did not go as intended and ultimately would be there for advice at that point. It seemed to us that people's creativity was being released when they were given opportunities – leadership opportunities – to get on with things that were personal to them and to which they had a personal commitment. This seemed to lead to what Barth (2003: 64) called 'profound learning'. The excitement of individuals discovering this came out in many examples in numerous interviews.

One principal of a large secondary school in the west of England said:

It took a while but with the staff I have now, I am happy for them to make all the key decisions about individual students, some of whom have nil support outside of school. After all, they know that individual through and through and I know they will be acting for the right reasons in that student's interests. I'll back them if it doesn't quite work and we'll talk about why it didn't. I and the school supply the professional guidelines and general policies and then it's over to them. Sometimes it is tougher like this for me personally, easier to give orders!

For such attitudes to exist in a school, there has to be a huge amount of trust between all those involved, and we now consider the ethos within which this trust and other elements thrive.

School Ethos

Simplistically, one could describe the ethos and atmosphere in the schools succeeding so well in difficult conditions, and working with children from poor and disadvantaged backgrounds, as being busy and cheerful. The two characteristics that struck one in walking round and talking with both learners and staff were those of industry and smiles. Of course there were exceptions, with worried faces and much concentration, but overall there were very few sulks! Another feature was the mixture of noise and quiet! Here was a hubbub of activity and there, peace in a room, only broken by the scratching of pens – and heads – or keyboard tapping. Such a setting for education is not achieved easily or quickly, and our interviews with leaders, staff and learners lead us to believe that the main factors in achieving this working atmosphere include the following:

- *Equity and trust*: Schools are complex places in the reality of daily life and ethical dilemmas regularly face leaders and staff about each other and their learners. Tensions will arise between the needs of the community as a whole and those of the individual learner (after all, some teachers see this as a daily issue in their classrooms). The best schools seemed to recognise this complexity and hence favoured the 'leadership at all levels' approach, as described earlier, to manage such tensions on an individual basis. Only a climate of trust can enable this, and several senior leaders made it clear that such trust had had to be earned over a period. Only in communities where people felt that equity existed could this trust occur. Such equity or fairness has to be overt and therefore to be seen clearly in the actions and behaviour within the school. Perhaps the best criterion is seen in situations which are unpleasant, and people are inclined to say, 'I don't like it at all, but it *is* fair!' (Middlewood and Abbott, 2017: 21). Without such trust and overt equity, the scope for 'being myself' for adults and children and young people is reduced and it becomes easier simply to do the same as the next person. In such contexts, learners quickly note that the systems and procedures appear to take priority over what they see as important for themselves as individuals.

- *Recognition and praise*: All the most successful schools placed huge emphasis on ensuring that recognition and praise for effort and achievement were regularly given. However, the key to effectiveness here seemed to be in the individuality of this recognition. Some of these schools had abandoned school-wide systems of rewards completely, while some others retained them in a modified form.

Steph, a principal in an urban high school in New Zealand, described her school's experience.

Case Example 7.1

'In my first three years as principal here, we tried various forms of rewards (and sanctions) systems, each time modifying the previous scheme after feedback from staff and students. The problem each time was the one of staff inconsistency, so perceived by both groups! "Mr X was very mean, and Mrs Y gives them (rewards) too liberally; Ms Z makes exceptions and that's not fair!" In the end, we thought – "Let's go for inconsistency!" Well, what I really mean is, let each member of staff decide who deserves praise or reward – trust their professional judgement. So now, if a teacher rewards a girl who has written ten words after doing none previously because the teacher thinks that deserves a reward, while others who produce much more do not, so be it. We say each learner is an individual so we should not make their efforts fit the system, the system should fit them. The interesting thing now is that those same complaints still crop up but now in an affectionate way, as an expression of knowing that teacher ("Mr Y is a real old meanie!") as an individual with that characteristic, and not as one who doesn't apply the rules properly!'

Not all the leaders felt the same as Steph. Some felt that they operated highly successful systems and were confident that they worked well for both staff and learners. In some of these schools, although our interviews with learners were limited, a few of them indicated satisfaction with the amount of praise and encouragement received, with a number suggesting that praise from their personal teacher outweighed any official recognition.

- *A 'no excuse' approach*: Underpinning the commitment in greatly disadvantaged schools to ensuring achievement was a refusal to accept any excuses for underachieving below what it was felt each individual was capable of. Several interviewees at all levels within schools stressed that failure was not tolerated except as something you could learn from. Tandi, a primary school principal in Limpopo in South Africa, said that she told both her staff and her learners regularly about her own personal failures. 'I tell them about all the mistakes I have made in my life and things that I tried to do and couldn't do, at first. I say I realised I would have to try another way and eventually found a way to do something. So when they fail or say they cannot do something, we try to get them to ask why they failed and how can you get it right or at least better next time. But – never give up!'

What was notable in these schools was the determination of all those involved to persist and not allow any sign of 'I can't do it' to appear! Of course, not everyone can do everything, but as soon as a learner appeared to resign themselves to not succeeding, someone would say in effect, 'Yes, you can do it; let us sort out how.'

- *Understanding but not pity*: Successful leaders showed an intense awareness and understanding of many learners' vulnerabilities caused by their home circumstances. In some cases, this came from the leader's own personal upbringing where they had had to fight to achieve their current position against considerable odds. Parker (1997) in research for the National College of School Leadership found that several of the successful school leaders' life histories involved the person concerned being determined to give learners from poor backgrounds a better chance to succeed at school, so as not to repeat their own struggles. Daniel, a secondary school principal in a London borough, was typical of such people. He said, 'I came from a working-class home where my father had left when I was born. I am black and my mother is white, and we met huge prejudices in my earlier school days. I was badly behaved and a rebel against any authority. My mother tried her best for me, but it was difficult with very little money in the home. Several of my friends from primary school dropped out of education and were always truanting from secondary school. I watched them get into trouble with the law and didn't want to do that to my mother. I woke up to my possibilities when a couple of teachers told me how good I was at history. I got completely hooked on that and related subjects, started to get some praise and good marks and made up my mind to help my family by success in education. After I got my history degree and became a teacher, I vowed always to work in so-called 'poor' schools and ever since, I was – and am – committed to helping them succeed by showing them what they are capable of. I never forget what nearly happened to me.'

However, understanding and in some cases empathetic leaders and staff may be of learners' difficulties, they were determined to show that just being sorry for them is not enough. As a teacher in Daniel's school said in an interview, 'My heart goes out to them with what some of them have to put up with – *but* – pity can breed self-pity and that will never get them out of those situations. So we sympathise of course, and then drive them on to show themselves and everyone else that they *can* achieve despite those things. Why? Because they are who they are, not where they are, or where they're from. Well, that's how I'd put it!'

Paul, a primary school deputy head teacher in a London borough with high levels of deprivation, made the point that, although it is true that for many children from chaotic and dysfunctional homes, school can be their only refuge, it does not help them if the school's only task is just to provide that security. He said, 'What is the point in simply doing that, if, when they leave school, they simply go back into those awful lives? All the school will have done for them is to postpone it – and your school years in the end are only making up a small part of one's whole lifetime. We must help them to see that they can achieve what they're capable of while they have this security and then they learn that when they leave school having some form of structure or order in their lives is essential for doing good things. You might even say we help them to see that chaos is dangerous!'

- *Belief in everyone's ability to achieve*: No matter how extreme the adverse circumstances were of any child in these schools, the leaders – and their staffs – were completely committed to believing that every single individual was capable of achievement. Perhaps the words of Andrew, the head teacher of a school down on the south coast of England, which had received parentless immigrant and refugee children on the school roll, encapsulate this well:

> I would write no one off, even when they have written themselves off. Some of our children have come from unimaginable situations; been found floating in a boat at sea, virtually alone, had their homes attacked or burned down, been abused, starved, lost everything. They are still who they are inside. We

set out to find who that person is, we believe in their potential and try to get them to believe in it. Sometimes it is a long, slow process, but it is always worth doing. Tiny steps are taken at first and early on, yes, it may be more about human compassion than education, but as they have to adapt to completely new contexts, that is a huge learning curve and then we can build on that. Eventually, we find of course that there is the same range as everywhere – some academically gifted, some with practical skills, some who are just what you might call entrepreneurial. This is all done in a new language too! We are able to keep saying to them – 'Look what you have learned already!'

Sadie, a principal of a community school in a poor area of New York, said, 'If we don't try to do something for these kids, it is as if we are saying that we blame them because they are poor! I don't understand that. I don't get it! Even when you feel it might be their parents' fault that they are where they are, it's certainly not the children's fault! I thought that's what people came into education and teaching for!' But, for heaven's sake, push them as hard as you would the kids from rich homes – there's no other way!'

In a different school in another deprived area of New York, we were told by Chas, the principal, that the culture or ethos had been the main focus when the leadership changed five years earlier. In Case example 7.2, he describes this change:

Case Example 7.2

'I hadn't realised till I'd been here for a little while, and talking to students, just how few expected not to complete their schooling! Quite a few would be assuming when asked about the future – "Oh, I don't suppose I'll be here then anyway." What was worse-most of these didn't seem to mind or were resigned to it. A few were indignant but not so many. It didn't take in-depth research to see that most of these were from more deprived backgrounds, and largely Latino or black students. Like they were saying, "What else do you expect?"

We have a far smaller drop-out rate now and it's down to two things, I think. One, getting them, virtually all of them, to believe that *we* believed in them, that *they* could succeed. How did we do that? Change the whole dynamic of teacher–student relationships, so the students didn't think they were just part of a mass of people, but that the teachers knew them individually and cared about them as individuals. At first, the students (and some teachers!) were sceptical, but now it's a different place to be in. and by the way, there's much less violence, vandalism and very few drug offences. I would advocate that way round. The other of course, is coming in heavy on those things and cleaning up, then showing people it's a decent place. I know what I think is the best way!'

- *Pressure and urgency*: Whilst there are major concerns in various countries about the debilitating effects of stress on both teachers and learners, primarily in those contexts where governments place huge emphasis on schools achieving high success in measurable areas such as tests and examinations, it is also known that a certain amount of stress is essential for human beings to operate effectively (Donaldson-Feilder et al. (2011). In these successful schools where we describe the atmosphere as busy (see above), the sense of urgency to improve and the pressure on everyone to achieve this improvement was palpable. In interviews, senior leaders regularly used words such as 'relentless' or 'remorseless' to describe their continuous focus on learning. 'Everything we do has to be about their learning', was a typical statement from one principal of a primary school in Birmingham in the English Midlands. This was a place, where at the end of the school day, as the children left the premises, staff, both teachers and assistants, stood by the doors and asked pupils at random, 'What have you learned today?' It was explained that this was deliberately not done systematically, because the children would soon have learned stock replies, even prepared ones. But it had become part of the school's own way of doing things and answers could relate to any aspect of school life, ranging from something learned in maths to how to keep out of trouble. What was interesting, however, was that the children were encouraged to ask the staff the same question, and that included all leaders! One teacher new to the school commented that, 'I thought it odd at first – a bit of a gimmick! But after a while, I came to realise that if I did not know what I had learned that day, then I might as well not have bothered coming!'

If there is a temptation to see this stress on learning as relentless, it should be noted that almost every one of these successful schools offered specific 'off timetable' periods when normal routines were abandoned and special activities were arranged, with an emphasis on doing something different – perhaps once a term or once a year, as in Case example 7.3.

Case Example 7.3

A medium-sized secondary school in a run-down area of a large city in Scotland has now established that each summer term, it cancels normal timetabled classes for the whole school. All learners and all staff become part of various teams which compete over five days in a range of activities, some physical, some mental, some slightly comic. The activities are carefully planned weeks in advance by staff and more senior learners, with a brief to ensure involvement for all ages, all abilities and all personalities – all prior to any teams being chosen.

Thus, one year this could involve organising a circus, running a business, orienteering, solving puzzles, playing sports that one had never tried before, and so on.

The aim is to stretch everyone by involving people in a new area where they could discover new skills and new things about themselves. It is seen as exhausting, frantic, stimulating and enjoyable. There is careful evaluation and feedback each time of each activity, and this is scrutinised to enable the next year's week to be even more fit for purpose. The deputy principal has said that the two key things sought in evaluation were – what learning had taken place and whether anyone had been made to feel uncomfortable in any activity, so that that activity could be modified or removed.

- *Sense of togetherness*: In these successful schools, there was an almost extraordinary sense of 'We are all in this together' among the staff. In the most successful schools, this sense of a shared community to which everyone contributed, came from the staff, the learners, and many of the parents. One instance that we recall arose when talking to an administrative assistant in a school in one of the most deprived urban districts we visited in South Africa. We asked her what her actual job was. With a smile, she replied, 'The same as everyone else who works here – making sure these kids learn enough to get out of here and make a better life for themselves and the future!' Any other job description seemed pointless to us after that! In such communities, every single person plays an important part, no matter how apparently minor their role appears on paper. We recall a school janitor in another South African school telling us that he took pride in keeping the school buildings clean and tidy because he wanted 'these kids to have pride in this place and then I'll think they'll do better, you know, learn better. Most of their homes aren't very clean so being here helps them see what it can be like to be in a nice place.'

Relationships and Communications with Staff

It was very clear that the effective leaders of these schools had developed networks of relationships within the school (as they had outside the school – see Chapter 10 on Community involvement). These leaders were never office-bound, but constantly interacting with all the personnel in the school. They had built up or were building up a good knowledge of each member of the school community as an individual. Walking with them around a school, whether in class, corridor, playing fields, or open areas, they seemed to know everyone by name and had the ability to comment or ask about something relevant to that person on a scale that was so noticeable to the outsider.

'How did you get on at the dentist's on Monday?'

'Is your wife feeling better now?'

'Did your son get that apprenticeship?'

'I see your team won on Saturday!'

The extent to which such individual knowledge of other people builds trust and respect is hard to quantify, but it seemed significant to us. Of course, it takes time for his to happen and it cannot be done quickly, but in interviews, several leaders made clear that this was a specific aim of theirs and at least two had particular strategies for ensuring their personal knowledge of people was up to date. One principal told us that at the beginning of each week (Monday morning), 20 minutes was spent with senior leaders exchanging all news they had about personal issues, all of which were carefully noted down! As one principal acknowledged, 'Sometimes, though not often, I get it wrong – whoops! Then I admit my mistake and spend the next few minutes getting the correct news, so I end up knowing even more!'

Slater (2004: 58) drew on research evidence to suggest that 'knowing people is crucial in developing the trust and respect that characterize collaborative relationships', and it seems that fundamental to success in this 'knowing' is effective communication. The two most important elements of this communicating appeared to be speaking and listening. In this age of technological services such as email, smart phones, Skype, and all kinds of social media, it was clear to us that, whilst these were important, the key factors influencing leaders' relationships with staff (and indeed with learners and parents) were their ability to listen to and to talk with people. Listening is perhaps the most important of all and Goleman (1998) warned that leaders who did not or could not listen were likely to be seen as indifferent or even uncaring. Interviews with school staff about leaders' effectiveness regularly referred to their being 'a good listener'. Active listening is a skill that goes beyond hearing of course, to what may be hidden meanings and also involves the reading of non-verbal or body language.

Also, the effective leaders seemed adept at adapting their language and inter-action according to the other participants, and skilled at teasing out sometimes more hidden motivations in the other person. This whole area of the language of school leaders merits a research project in itself, but our interviews with leaders and those they interacted with certainly gave clear evidence of its crucial importance in building relationships across the school.

Relationships with Learners

Several of the points made in the section above were equally true here in considering leaders' relationships with school learners, including communication skills and getting to know the learners as individual people. Whilst it was clearly not possible for the principal of a large secondary school to know the name and details of every single learner, some principals showed remarkable abilities in this field. Whilst walking around the school and grounds, they addressed many learners by name, and made social comments to large numbers, always as individuals. Whilst some comments were 'small talk', many were personal:

'Things getting better in maths now, I hear. Keep it up!'
'Well done, Carmen! I'm hearing good things about you from Mrs X.'
'How's your mother getting on in the new job, Rhania?'
'Come and tell me about the new band you're in, Marlene.'

These leaders were at great pains to receive information about each learner's progress, particularly in social, emotional and behavioural areas, knowing that these were key to any improvement in academic development. As one secondary principal noted:

It is important that all learners feel that the good things about them are being passed on to what I might call higher authority, and perhaps some of the 'bad' things are being dealt with by those staff at the level where they build a close empathetic relationship with them. So, you see, I have the easy job!

When addressing groups of learners, especially on formal occasions, it was noticeable that senior leaders used very little abstract language, and made few references to school values in those phrases. They tended to speak in concrete terms, so their focus was on what people had done, how they had behaved, and the consequences of these actions. It was in this way that they communicated the values that the school espoused – what Davies (2006: 13) called ' demonstrable values'.

One principal in a school in Limpopo, South Africa, said, 'I would like to think that, when a visitor comes here, they can see what we believe in, without us having to tell them. That's what we are aiming for anyway.'

The other noticeable thing about these leaders was the way they projected themselves both to staff and often to learners, as also being learners. Dom was a principal of a large school in a US West Coast city and it was his second principalship. He describes this in Case example 7.4

Case Example 7.4

'I made an error at the start and I should have known better! I rather assumed that what I had successfully done at my first school where I'd been the leader would work here too. Despite my experience and reading, I ignored that, and it took some setbacks to remind me that every context is unique, however similar it may look to another.

In my first school, I had, right from the start, used my powers of persuasion to get the staff and parents and students to "see it my way"! I was successful and the school prospered and everyone was happy. That's a bit simple, but overall, that was how it was when I look back.

Here, my eloquence and my persuasive powers seemed to fall on deaf ears and after a month or two of getting nowhere, word reached me that I was seen as arrogant and knowing it all. Me!

Looking back, I know I had forgotten to build relationships first before working out how to negotiate my way ahead. Because I was seen as arrogant (I'm not!), my ideas were automatically rejected without a hearing. As I thought about it, I realised that is what I, when young, had done – I had rejected ideas from people whom I didn't like. It's normal then!

So – I started again. Basically, I swallowed my pride and went around, listening to people, especially the students, heard their moans and groans, heard their ideas – including some crazy ones – and slowly built up a picture of them, their environments and my mantra was often – "I'm learning! I'm learning!" When I eventually started putting forward new proposals, I could present them in a way that recognised their way of looking at things and suggesting how my idea might move us all on. It took longer than in my first school, but actually, I feel there's a stronger foundation in changes made here than in the other place. There was a widespread joke about me that I pretended not to notice for a long time – the students used to say, out of hearing, "Well, he's only a learner, remember!" When at a staff meeting, a teacher told me about it, I was able to say that I took it as a compliment, and they should all do the same!'

Dom was possibly referring to Thomson's (2008) four-stage model of negotiation in his account, but the more important point was his honest admission about learning – and about the mistake he made – one of the key ways of learning of course!

Qualities and Values of Leaders Seen in Action

We will return to some of the issues identified in this chapter in Chapter 12. Here, we may say that these highly effective leaders possessed some qualities in abundance, of which the key ones seemed to be:

- A consistently empathetic approach to these learners from hugely disadvantaged contexts. They understood that their behaviour was caused by factors external to the school, and was therefore not personal to the school or its personnel. Consequently, they and their staff tended to depersonalise tricky situations as they arose in school, and dealt with them accordingly.

- The difficulties of the students' outside-school context was never to be used as an excuse for poor learning performance or unacceptable behaviour; it could be an explanation but not an excuse.

- They were insistent that every learner was an individual and was not to be judged by others' behaviour or attitude towards them.

- They believed strongly that dealing with and improving the emotional development of the children and young people and helping them grow in self-belief would, with very good teaching, lead to raised attainment in learning.

- Above all, they strove to put strong and positive relationships at every level at the heart of the school as a community. Relationships between leaders and staff, staff and staff, staff and learners, learners and learners – all these were seen to be central to the growth of everyone as an individual, as a group member and as a member of the school community.

This quality of building relationships, so evident in all these leaders, is key to what Harris and Jones (2029: 268) see as their success in 'building collaboration and consensus' – the second of our principles, and the subject of the next chapter.

Summary

This chapter has:

- outlined some relevant models of school and educational leadership
- stressed the significance of leadership existing at all levels within school
- explained how leaders are important in establishing the appropriate school ethos
- examined leaders' relationships and communications with staff
- examined leaders' relationships with learners
- noted the qualities displayed by successful school leaders and their emphasis on values in action

Chapter 8
Collaboration

Introduction

In this chapter on the second of our four key principles, we focus on collaboration. As we noted in the previous chapter, leadership is never effective when it is viewed as a one-person process, and the most success comes when leadership is shared among as many people as possible. This chapter develops that concept across a wider area.

The notion of collaborative practice is fundamental to effective leadership, staff development and community involvement. Schools working in isolation, however successful they may be, are not contributing to the overall development of raising achievement for all learners. Jerrim, Greany and Perrera (2018) in their comparative study of educational disadvantage in England and other countries, found that segregation between schools along with selection by ability are noticeably absent from those countries which achieve high performance and have equity in the provision of education for all. Just as successful schools have effective collaboration practices within them, so different schools, their leaders and their staff also need to work together for this purpose. We will focus on ways in which collaboration can lead to an improvement in the education system and bring about better outcomes for disadvantaged students. In particular, this chapter will:

- discuss the reasons why schools work together
- identify the ways in which schools work together
- explore the impact of collaboration
- consider collaboration within a school
- provide an extended Case example of a school where collaboration is at the core of their activities

Why do Schools Work Together?

In this book we are concerned with developing strategies that will help schools to deliver improvements in their performance to bring about improved education for disadvantaged students. Middlewood, Abbott and Robinson (2018: 6) have identified a variety of reasons why schools might work together depending on their circumstances and the broader education system they find themselves operating in:

- education is still widely, if not universally, regarded as a human entitlement and therefore seen as predominantly part of a public or state provision. Within national education systems there is still a focus on public service and a recognition that institutions should cooperate to benefit from the system as a whole
- statutory regulations imposed by a funding agency which could be either local or central government

- a realisation that 'weaker' schools could benefit from the skills and experience of more 'successful' schools
- economies of scale to provide improved service and choice
- financial pressures
- sharing of leadership skills and staff development opportunities
- as a form of defensive reaction against perceived external threats
- in some cases, schools may be compelled to work together because they are controlled by an external body

There is no one reason why schools choose to work together, and it is often a combination of factors that create the conditions for schools to work together. In many countries, such as England, the United States and Australia, greater school autonomy and the reduction of local government control has meant that schools have taken the initiative to work together rather than operate in isolation even if there is some element of competition. In many developing countries schools choose to work together out of necessity because they often lack basic infrastructure. If, for example, only one school has access to specialised facilities it makes sense to share to make those resources available to all. Research and consultancy work we carried out with head teachers in one of the poorest regions of Tanzania is illustrated in Case example 8.1. There was a lack of basic resources, many children were lost from the education system, and standards were low despite some heroic efforts from school leaders, the teachers, students and the wider community (Middlewood, Abbott, Netshandama and Whitehead, 2017).

Case Example 8.1

George was the experienced principal of a secondary school and was involved in training and support for new secondary school principals. He had also developed extensive links with the local primary schools. He spoke of the benefits of working in collaboration with other schools:

'Of course, I'm interested in my school and doing the best I can for my students; that has to be my priority. I enjoy being able to support others. As you know we lack many basic facilities across the region, and this is an area with a lot of rural poverty, so I think we have to go beyond self-interest if we're going to raise standards. It's local but also regional and national. We lack so much, and our students face all sorts of pressures to drop out of the system, we have to do all we can to help them succeed. So, if I can pass on my skills to other principals, I'm happy to do it. It makes sense to work with our primary schools, we have better facilities and we want to encourage children to stay in the system. We have to do all we can to make it safe and normal for them to go on to secondary schools. We have to develop the system and that will eventually benefit the students, all students. We need cooperation and commitment from everyone to improve the system. There has to be better regional planning and setting of priorities with schools working together. Staffing is a real problem for us, getting enough teachers of the right quality. Many teachers become demotivated because of the heavy workloads, large classes and poor facilities, especially professional support. If I can help out with professional development, it will help everyone in the system. I firmly believe by collaborating we can create a better education system for all.

As well as working with large groups I often work on a one-to-one basis on specific problems with other principals. I'm currently working with a relatively new principal as a mentor, just to give him the opportunity to have someone to share with. Whatever it is, it is about improving the systems for our staff but most importantly for our students who need all the help they can get. We cannot afford to be precious about what we do and who take help from.'

George highlights the importance of collaboration to improve the education system as a whole for all students. In this part of Tanzania, there was an acceptance of collaboration as a means to achieve an improved education system which would benefit the country as a whole, but it would also help individual students. In more prosperous countries there might be less emphasis on improving the education system as a whole, but the end result of collaboration should be the same to improve outcomes for individual students.

In countries such as England, Australia and the United States there will tend to be a greater focus on individual projects and small groups of schools working on particular issues and problems. This is often in response to one school being perceived to be performing less well than another. The identification of stronger schools helping weaker schools is not without some difficulty. There may well be resentment and, of course, a feeling from the weaker school that staff in the other school do not fully understand the context in which they are working. This type of relationship will only succeed if there is communication and mutual respect between both parties. Dialogue will be important, and it is important that a professional working relationship is established. However, it is easy to see how this type of arrangement might not work out in practice. Case example 8.2 gives an illustration of collaboration that did not work and what the school did to mitigate the situation:

Case Example 8.2

Lydia, head teacher of a primary school situated in a deprived area of a large city in the West Midlands of England, talked about a collaboration between a number of primary schools and a local secondary school:

'When we started it seemed like a good idea – we could all learn together. The secondary school had been on an upward trajectory and had improved all round since the new head teacher came in. They had established a real positive presence locally; results had gone up and their reputation especially with parents had soared. We had parents who previously would not have wanted to send their child there, but that had changed. It seemed like a win for everyone if we collaborated more closely. However, before long we realised that it just wasn't working. Although the secondary school had lots of staff, facilities and resources they didn't seem to get it, our issues and concerns. There did appear to be a real gulf. At times, my staff felt patronised and they would come back from joint meetings feeling it had been a complete waste of time. When we raised it with the second-ary head, she just seemed to brush it off – it was like we were there just to feed their school. So, we moved much more towards working together as a group of primary schools. We've maintained a relationship with the secondary school as we have to, especially for the sake of our pupils, but as a group of primary schools we have become quite close and share all sorts of things. Individual staff have estab-lished really good professional relationships and there's a lot going on; sometimes I'm the last to find out! I do believe our collaboration has helped a lot of children and we've been able to do so much more for some very deprived families. Funnily enough, the secondary school will get the benefit from it because our standards have risen and we're sending them fewer problems. The real benefit has been for our children because what we are able to do as a school and as individual teachers is so much better than it was before.'

Ways in which Schools Work Together

In practice there will be different level of collaboration between schools. Chapman (2015: 48–49) has identified a range of 'collaborative activity' based on a hierarchy of collaboration:

1 Association. This is a traditional model based on the involvement of a local authority or district to coordinate the process and is restricted to attendance at meetings and continuing professional development events.

2 Co-operation. A greater level of involvement which involves the opportunity to share current information and materials on a restricted basis.

3 Collaboration. This is based on the need to deal with specific issues and problems. It is commonly associated with a successful school supporting one that is perceived to be failing and will involve shared knowledge and resources and restricted opportunities to create new information and materials.

4 Collegiality. A deeper and longer lasting relationship is developed which involves agreement around outcomes and approaches. Information is pooled and new material is developed to benefit all the partners.

In practice most examples of schools working together will involve a mixture of the types of activity described by Chapman. Many of these arrangements will evolve over time and often will develop as a consequence of specific issues. The aim of these types of initiative is to bring about school improvement through shared leadership, knowledge and practice (Hargreaves, 2010). There are a number of international examples of these types of collaboration between schools. For example, in the United States, Farrell, Woohlstetter and Smith (2012) have reported that the charter organisational model offers opportunities for collaboration and for schools to gain economies of scale. In our research for this book, we increasingly found models that reflected Chapman's collaboration and collegiality approaches. In Case example 8.3 we consider the example of two primary schools in the east of England that had developed a close working relationship.

Case Example 8.3

Delia is the head teacher of one of the primary schools in the study:

'Our nearest primary school had recently had a new head teacher and I was approached by a community leader who I knew on their governing body if I'd like to speak to him about what we do and to provide a bit of mentorship. We both take children into our schools from across a fairly large, deprived area. There are high levels of unemployment and deprivation with lots of social problems. It's difficult to break the cycle, parents who've had their own bad experience of school at times can be hostile, that is often a major obstacle to overcome. Both schools face similar problems and of course our context is pretty much the same. Over the last six years, since I was appointed, we've seen consistent improvement in performance, I suppose we've become a bit of a role model especially in working with children from deprived backgrounds. We get lots of visitors, like you, looking at what we do! The other school has not done as well, and this was their third head teacher since I've been here. I wasn't sure about doing it and it was a difficult first meeting because I'm not sure either of us were clear about the purpose. I told him I was there to help if he needed it and I was hoping to learn a few things that might be useful for me and my school as well. He later admitted to me he was worried I was going to tell him what to do and his school might become be taken over by us. However, since that first difficult meeting, things have gone from strength to strength. It started off as support, but it has really developed over the last 18 months, and we've now got a great working relationship. We both know we can pick up the phone and talk over any issues. I've learnt a lot as well and we've gone from just the two of us working together to involvement throughout the schools. It started at senior leadership level and then moved on to curriculum coordinators and class teachers. We've done joint things on assessment, subject resources, working with parents and we've collaborated with a range of organisations on setting up and running a food bank from both schools. There have been some strong relationships developed between the schools, it obviously helps that both schools are working in the same environment. We've also done joint things, such as theatre and museum trips, many of them designed to provide a broader experience for our most deprived kids. The next step, if we can secure sufficient funding, is a joint residential trip to the seaside. It's unbelievable but many of our children have never been to the seaside, even though it's only 60 miles away. We're confident that what we're doing is having a really beneficial impact on all our children, but especially those from the most deprived backgrounds. I can honestly say we have all benefited from the process. I was lucky that the school structure allowed for this type of development to take place, it's been encouraged from both schools and reflects the greater freedoms we have been given as head teachers to control what we do and how we operate.

Case example 8.3 sets out the benefits from two schools working closely together. What started as a fairly limited collaboration has grown to become a major part of both schools' activities, but they are still two very separate and individual institutions. The catalyst for the development was two individual head teachers establishing a positive working relationship and accepting that to improve the chances of disadvantaged students they could achieve more together. Personal relationships are important, but it is also worth recognising that both individuals had a strong commitment to closing the attainment gap and to bring about whole-school improvement. In addition to the United Kingdom, initiatives of this nature can be found in many countries such as Australia, Canada, the United States, parts of Africa and Asia. Changes in the way in which schools are structured, governed and led have made collaboration easier, see for example: Policy Exchange (2009); Chapman (2015) and Middlewood, et al. (2018). Governments across the world have encouraged greater school autonomy whilst at the same time implementing polices designed to facilitate formal and informal collaboration between schools in the belief that it will help to raise standards. Schools that are perceived as being successful are often encouraged, in some cases through financial inducements, to work with less successful schools to develop and promote best practice. There are a number of examples of this, for example in England the Teaching Schools initiative, in the United States, the laboratory schools, in Australia, demonstration schools (Middlewood, et al., 2018).

The Impact of Collaboration between Schools

As we have seen earlier in the chapter, the decision to collaborate between schools is taken in the belief that working together will improve education standards and lead to a number of other benefits including the provision of additional resources, increased opportunities for professional development and individual support. This will be achieved, for example, through economies of scale, a pooling of expertise and a programme of mutual support. In some cases, this could be through a central government initiative or, as we outlined above, a more localised approach as we described in Case example 8.3. Staff and students in schools that decide to collaborate need to see a positive return to their efforts and there has to be an effective evaluation of the process to determine whether it is worthwhile. For the purposes of this book we are concerned with the impact on disadvantaged students from a collaboration between schools and colleges, but in some senses the benefits will apply to any situation. A positive collaboration between schools has the possibility to impact on the:

- level of overall resource available through economies of scale
- overall quality of staff through increased experience and exposure to different ideas and approaches
- type and range of teaching materials available
- teaching and learning and assessment strategies employed by the schools participating
- type of monitoring and record keeping employed by schools and colleges
- overall quality of data and use of data to monitor student progress
- range of experience available to staff and students
- access to research and information
- availability of a wider range of support services and networks
- access to specialised facilities

If a collaboration does not deliver a range of benefits to all the parties involved, then it will be necessary to stop the initiative. It is not a good use of staff time and effort to continue with something that is not creating added value. It may just be that the collaboration was not properly developed and that it lacked clear aims and objectives. Political concerns may also have played a part, which is why it is important to ensure that the reasons for the collaboration are robust and mutually agreed. However, encouraging schools and colleges to work together more closely is likely to bring about benefits to all parties in the long term, but especially for students from disadvantaged backgrounds.

Collaboration within a School

We have looked at the ways and reasons why schools decide to collaborate. There are obvious benefits from a collaborative approach between institutions and there will be increasing opportunities for schools to collaborate. We will now turn to consider collaboration within an institution and explore some of the benefits that can arise when a school develops a collaborative approach across all aspects of its work. Generally, collaboration within a school or college will be a positive activity because it will provide opportunities for the sharing of good practice across the institution and can play a significant part in staff development. Working with others, reducing any sense of isolation for staff and being aware of how pupils are performing across a range of subject areas will be likely to lead to improved outcomes for students.

We consider some of the benefits collaboration with a range of outside agencies can bring in Chapter 10, Community involvement. In this section of this chapter we focus on staff within a school or college. Within a school we would stress that it is important that all staff are involved in collaborative activities. That is not to say that all staff have to be involved in every aspect of a student's school life, but there should not be any discrimination between different staff within a school. There will be occasions when both teaching and non-teaching staff are involved in an activity; at other times it might just be the teaching staff or support staff. It will also be important to keep governors informed of the general approach and direction of what a school or college is doing to close the attainment gap. This is good practice but takes on added importance when a school or college is inspected by an external body.

What is important is that there is a process and a culture that facilitates a collaborative approach across a school or college. All areas of the institution have to be able to work together to improve student outcomes, if silos are allowed to develop this could undermine effective practice. If collaboration is likely to be of benefit across a school or college more generally it is reasonable to assume that it will take on added significance for those students from disadvantaged backgrounds. It is important that teachers and non-teaching staff are aware of the problems faced by individual students. Where there are large numbers of disadvantaged students, common approaches to deal with a range of issues can be developed and staff can employ a consistent and coherent approach. Examples could include common teaching and learning strategies or the establishment of certain protocols when dealing with parents. Collaborative practice across the school or college will ensure a consistency of approach and ensure that there is clear guidance on actions and responsibilities. We spent a period of time at a large secondary academy school situated on the coast of eastern England, where we focused on the issue of collaboration externally and internally. In Case example 8.4, Rebecca the head teacher explains what internal collaboration means in her school and how it works in practice.

Case Example 8.4

'It's fair to say we have our share of problems! There's a lot of disadvantage locally built up over many years with the decline of traditional employment and although tourism is important it's seasonal and the work is often low paid. People who come to the area for a holiday don't see the deprivation. Historically there has not been a tradition of belief that education is a means of improving your life chances. For example, participation rates going on to higher education are still fairly low, it's not helped by not having a local university. When we see reports of costal area students being well behind their counterparts in other parts of the country we fit into that category – our attainment gap is for some students totally unacceptable. We have a large number of pupil premium students and a lot of students who have quite poor home circumstances and of course a number who do not have English as a first language. That's not to say we haven't been doing some great work and things are definitely improving at my school anyway. You've seen our data and things are getting better. I know you asked me about collaboration within the school, but it's important to set out the context we're operating in. I'd also add we collaborate closely with a number of external partners including two local primary schools and the other two schools in our MAT.

I'm not sure I'd use the word collaboration; I'd describe it more as communication. What we're trying to do is to encourage everyone, and I mean everyone, to work together with common goals to improve outcomes for all our students. I know you are primarily interested in our disadvantaged students, but I believe it's important we have a whole school approach. Yes, we do some, lots really, additional things for the most disadvantaged but I'm concerned about every child. So that's the principle, getting everyone onside and buying into our approach. Recognising we have to close the attainment gap but not forgetting the rest of the students. It starts from the appointment of staff; we're looking for people who are open, and want to work in a collaborative manner, no hiding and shutting the classroom door here. I cannot pretend that's always easy because staff recruitment is often difficult in a school like this. We have made some great appointments, and they have clearly bought into the ethos we're trying to embed. We have formal structures in place, but we are very much about making sure no one is on their own. There should always also be someone to support and to work alongside. It's a culture of cooperation and to use your word, collaboration, and that goes right across the school.

I suppose the other starting point is data, we have huge amounts of data, every school has, but it's being smart about how you use it. Unless it leads to something, data is useless for its own sake. We make sure data is easy to understand and is widely shared to all relevant parties, there's no point in not doing that. So presentation and distribution are important, I'm lucky I have some great staff who are really good at presenting the data, making sure it's consistent so even I can understand it! It's also about tracking and keeping a trail of how an individual student is doing and of course data has to bring forward actions.

We need to be able to see clearly how a student is doing, what we are doing to improve things and whether it has worked. It's important that all the relevant staff are aware of that process and are kept informed. It's very easy for disadvantaged children to slip out of sight, we have the data and processes to make sure that doesn't happen. Staff are aware and clear about their responsibilities and we keep track of what is happening to each individual. It's time consuming but worth it in the end, when you see someone succeed against the odds.

We are very strong on encouraging staff to work together, and to promote common approaches. I think it really helps in a school like this to foster the feeling that we are all in this together. That's important at every level and we don't want to see a them-and-us approach. Some of our students have such a raw deal and their lives are difficult, it's up to us to do what we can to offset that, so we need to be seen to be working together and to promote coherent approaches. We do not want to give mixed messages and of course working together should prevent any duplication of effort or people going off message. Let's make the best use of the scarce resources we have. So, collaboration is important to us as a school and we encourage it in the classroom, across subject departments, within our pastoral system and of course at senior management level. We have to recognise that ultimately, it's the people in the classroom who are going to make things work or not. So, making sure there is clear communication and support for them is essential to ensure we can do the best we can. I like to think we support our staff especially through staff development, but it's important if they learn something they come back to school and share it more widely.'

This was to be the end of this Case example but, we were fortunate enough to be able to speak via a video link to Rebecca again in September 2020 during the COVID-19 pandemic, just as the school was fully reopening, to see how her school had responded to the lockdown measures that had been introduced and how this had impacted on collaboration within the school. Her words follow:

'Well, it's been an interesting few months to say the least! As I'm sure you can imagine, things are very different to when you visited us last year. Stuff seems to have been happening daily, but we're still here and have welcomed back all our staff and students to something as close to normality as we can get it. We've made great use of technology during the last few months. As a staff we've had close collaboration through virtual meetings and frequent progress updates. We've continued to monitor students as best we can. I have to say some of the response to online learning has not been great, especially amongst the most disadvantaged students. We've noticed in the short time we've been back at school that many of our students have slipped back and if anything, the attainment gap is now wider. Some of our students have not yet reappeared, so we are following that up. So, during the time when we were in lockdown collaboration became even more important to keep everyone together and to be clear about what we were trying to do and how we were going to move forward.

We established clear protocols and responsibilities, which to be honest we've always done. Staff were clear about what was expected and how to achieve it. We provided lots of support, both technical but also from a personal point of view to make sure everyone was comfortable with what we were doing. It's been a very difficult time so it's important people felt they had support and someone to talk things through with. Sharing resources and developing materials through teams of people working together really came into its own and we've now got some great stuff online. What we have missed, of course, is the human touch and the ability to interact as a staff and most importantly with students and their families. If we hadn't been so strong on collaboration throughout the school as we were before lockdown we would have struggled even more. I have to say, despite everything we've done we have a lot of catching up to do to make up for the last six months. Collaboration has been maintained and in some cases improved, although it's been different to what we were used to and I am relieved to be back in a fairly full school and to try and get back to normal, whatever that might be.'

Conclusion

For social justice to occur, collaboration is a requirement, not simply a desirable option, because if it is undertaken in an effective way it can improve the quality of education and lead to improved outcomes for all students, but especially those from disadvantaged backgrounds. Collaboration can take a number of forms and is commonly found in successful and improving schools. Collaboration between schools is likely to become more commonplace and is seen as a key factor in bringing about school improvement, especially in semi-autonomous education systems such as the United States (Kolodny, 2014). In developing countries, the drive for collaboration will come from central and local government in an attempt to make the best possible use of scarce resources (Middlewood, et al. 2018). There is a strong desire to spread good practice and to learn from others. Increased collaboration will enhance that process.

Given the additional problems caused by the COVID-19 pandemic with UNESCO (2020) reporting that only half of the eligible school population will return to school classrooms in the new academic year (2020/21), and with the situation being even worse for the most vulnerable populations it would seem even more urgent to make the most of the restricted resources available. Greater collaboration across education systems, and between and within schools will be required to address the issue which has been described by Audrey Azoulay, Director-General of UNESCO as severe and which will lead to a situation in which 'several generations are facing the threat of school closures which concern hundreds of millions of students and lasted many months. This is an emergency for global education.'

In this chapter we have:

- discussed the reasons why schools work together
- identified the ways schools work together
- explored the impact of collaboration between schools
- considered collaboration within a school
- provided an extended Case example of a school where collaboration is at the core of their activity

Chapter 9
Staff Training and Development

Introduction

In this chapter we focus on the third of our key principles, staff training and development. It is important to recognise that staff training and development should not be restricted to a minority of staff and should be available to all staff at every level. Staff training and development has been at the core of the operations of all the schools we have investigated for our research for this book. We have observed a commitment to staff training and development by senior leadership and from each member of staff we have spoken to in every school and college we have visited. There has been a willingness to undertake professional development, both personal and organisational, as a key factor in developing and improving strategies designed to reduce the attainment gap in schools.

Abbott, Rathbone and Whitehead (2019: 1) have argued that 'the importance of high-quality teaching in ensuring an outstanding education system has long been recognised. As a consequence, there has been increased interest in many countries in how teachers are trained and are able to access professional development throughout their career.' In this chapter we will consider the major components of staff development. We will look at the importance of establishing a sound knowledge and experience of working with disadvantaged students as an integral part of initial teacher training. We will then go on to consider how Continuous Professional Development (CPD) can help to reduce the attainment gap through the use of teaching and learning strategies in the classroom designed to help students from poorer backgrounds. In particular we will focus on the use of practitioner research to develop innovative and grounded approaches to working with disadvantaged students. Middlewood and Abbott (2015: 3) claim that 'CPD and professional learning for staff has been identified as one of the key factors in school improvement, both in developed countries (Bolam et al., 2000) and developing countries (Dalin and Rust, 1996)'. This chapter will:

- discuss the role played by initial teacher training in preparing staff to work effectively with students from disadvantaged backgrounds
- consider the use of CPD to enable staff to develop strategies to improve opportunities for disadvantaged students
- explore the use of practitioner research as a means to contribute to the reduction the attainment gap

Initial Teacher Education

In many countries there has been an ongoing debate about how teachers are initially trained. There has been a movement away from higher education-based systems to those that place greater emphasis on school experience. A number of general themes have developed around the ways in which teachers are trained:

- trainee teachers spend more time in school engaged in teaching and working with pupils
- there is an increased role for schools and experienced teachers in areas such as selection, supervision and assessment
- an emphasis on high levels of subject knowledge for new entrants to the teaching profession
- a decline in the amount of theory trainee teachers are exposed to during their training
- a movement to teaching being seen as a vocational rather than a professional occupation
- identification of particular models of teaching and classroom management reducing the amount of experimentation and experience of alternative models
- centralised control of teacher education with a defined curriculum, including awareness of working with school students from disadvantaged backgrounds
- the imposition of national standards
- a decline in the influence of higher education institutions and their staff
- a national system of inspection with publication of reports and the development of league tables
- problems of attracting sufficient numbers of new teachers, especially in particular subject areas and in certain schools
- encouragement for new and alternative training providers to compete with existing institutions
- the development of different models and routes to become a teacher
- the growth of political interference in teacher education and practice

    (Adapted from Abbott, et al., 2019: 4)

It is not within the scope of this book to consider these changes in detail. They will have an impact on the teaching that is carried out in all schools, but especially in those with significant numbers of students from disadvantaged backgrounds. We have earlier raised some issues about the importance of selecting and recruiting the right staff to work with disadvantaged students. Many of the schools we visited reported staff shortages and the difficulty of recruiting specialist staff in areas such as maths and science. A number of the schools reported having to use non-specialist teachers to teach some classes, something that is likely to further disadvantage already disadvantaged students. Access to suitably qualified teachers should be a prerequisite in any education system, but teachers also have to be suitably motivated to work in disadvantaged schools. During their training they should be given access to a full range of schools to determine in which type of school they might want to work. Some teachers will find it more rewarding to work in more deprived areas; others may prefer schools with other types of challenge. Different countries, of course, operate different systems for trainee teacher practice placements, ranging from asking students to arrange their own placements to tightly controlled arrangements, ensuring they sample different teaching contexts. In the most deprived province of South Africa, the local university which provided teacher training told us that no trainees wanted to teach in rural schools, even in practice, because of the poor pay and conditions – and, of course, many of those schools suffer from rural poverty and general disadvantage. It is important that trainee teachers are made aware of the benefits of working in different schools and should be encouraged to explore all options. There is a danger as Sobel (2018: 12) claims that 'it remains an awkward fact that disadvantaged pupils have a tendency to drift into the bottom sets and stay there' (Hallam and Parsons, 2013). In such sets they are generally assigned the least experienced or lowest quality teachers in the school.' We would argue that any system of teacher training should pay special attention to the needs of disadvantaged school students and the realities of working in schools in deprived areas, in particular:

- During their training programme all trainee teachers should develop an awareness and understanding of the attainment gap.
- All trainee teachers should develop an understanding of the possible causes of the attainment gap and the policies that might be used to alleviate it.
- Trainee teachers should develop a range of teaching and learning strategies that are suitable for school students from deprived backgrounds.
- Trainee teachers should have the opportunity to train in schools in deprived areas with significant numbers of disadvantaged students.
- Upon competition of their training teachers should be encouraged to work in schools in disadvantaged areas.

As we outlined in Chapter 1, a number of organisations have been established to train teachers who will specifically work in the most disadvantaged schools. The best-known examples are in the United States, Teach for America, and in England and Wales, Teach First. There are examples of this type of organisation in many other countries as diverse as India and Australia. There is a clear motivation on the part of the staff involved and the participants to do something about improving the life chances of the most deprived children and make sure every child has the opportunity to succeed. We spoke with a teacher, Alice, who had trained through the Teach First route in a secondary school we visited in the south-west of England. Case example 9.1 gives an indication of her motivation for becoming a teacher.

Case Example 9.1

I hadn't really considered teaching as a career, but Teach First inspired me when I came across it at uni. When I read about what they do and their concern with child poverty and educational inequality, I knew it was something I wanted to do. I wanted to make a difference, and we're all committed to making a difference. I've come a long way since I first started as a very nervous teacher in front of a class of 30 who expected me to know what I was doing. That's one of the benefits of being with Teach First because you are in the classroom from day one after the summer school. It was a tough first year, but I felt I was really achieving something. I wanted to work with children from disadvantaged backgrounds and in a deprived area. I've been very fortunate through everything I've done, and I just wanted to give something back. You know pretty much what you are letting yourself in for, lots of hard work and some tough times but you get through it. I was helped by there being other Teach First participants in the school who were in exactly the same situation as me, and I was able to talk things over with them. At times, the school was pretty chaotic and there were staff shortages, but I got through it and I was sure I'd made the right decision to go into teaching. The support I got from my mentor and through the Teach First conference days was really valuable. Two years further on, I'm still really enjoying teaching, working with my students and supporting new Teach First participants who come into our school. I really do think with Teach First we can make a difference and do something about educational inequality. The schools I work in along with some other Teach First trained staff has seen significant improvement and I know we've had a positive impact on the students we work with. There are now over 10,000 Teach First Teachers right across the country and we are going to make things better and improve the life chances of young people.

Case example 9.1 provides an example of a person who entered the teaching profession to work with students from disadvantaged backgrounds and who was strongly committed to 'making a difference' to those young people. Earlier in the book we commented on the importance of appointing the right staff who are aware of the realities of working in schools in disadvantaged areas and who are motivated to close the attainment gap. Teachers who have been through the Teach First training route clearly understand those realities and are obviously motivated. It is beyond the scope of this book, to make a judgement about the quality and impact of Teach First, see for example Abbott et al. (2019). However, it is clear that large numbers of committed, highly qualified graduates with proper levels of support and training, going to work in schools in deprived areas could have a significant positive impact. We should not forget that other training routes will also provide opportunities for their trainee teachers to work with disadvantaged students. In Case examples 9.2 and 9.3 we give a broader perspective to the issues surrounding the training of teachers when we consider a primary and secondary school who have developed their own approach to the training and recruitment of teachers.

Case Example 9.2

In this example we recount the experience of Anup who was assistant head teacher with responsibility for continuing professional development and initial teacher training at a large secondary academy school in London, where the majority of students were in receipt of pupil premium:

'We have a real focus on professional development and support for our own staff; we are also are proud of what we can offer trainee teachers. Our school has particular challenges, a lot of our students are from disadvantaged backgrounds and do not have English as a first language. We are able to offer a broad range of experience to trainee teachers, and it's tough but we offer a lot of support. It's important to remember that they are not here to replace qualified teachers, they're here to learn. I know some schools do use their trainees to cover vacancies, but we wouldn't do that, because trainee teachers need proper support and mentoring especially in a school like this. We take trainee teachers from almost every route, Teach First, PGCE and school-based training. I have to say I find the PGCE trainees the best, because they do not come with a one-size-fits-all approach and they tend to be more creative in what they do. No one can doubt the commitment of the Teach First participants, although they can be one-dimensional, but they can hit the ground running and are high-quality graduates. We have also been keen to encourage our teaching assistants and learning support assistants to take one of the routes to gain qualified teacher status. This has really helped us with staff recruitment. The added benefit of this is that they are already up to speed with the ethos and culture of the school. They understand the demands of the school and the high aspirations we have for our students whatever their background. They know very well what they are getting themselves into. This certainly is the best route for us and of course they stay and, in my experience, go on to be very good teachers.'

Case Example 9.3

For this Case example, we visited a group of primary schools in eastern England who had established a School Direct programme with a university where the majority of the training takes place within the school. All the schools had a significant number of students from disadvantaged backgrounds with a minority not having English as a first language. Robyn, one of the head teachers in the consortium, summarised the reasons for the development of the programme:

'In some ways we are a strange mixture, because part of where we are located is very attractive and is quite rural. However, in the urban areas there are some high levels of deprivation and we also have pockets of rural poverty which is often not recognised. As a group of head teachers we often talk about the problems of recruiting and retaining staff and, of course, we've been competing for the same small pool. Recruitment to this part of the world is not easy, it's a bit out of the way and people are often reluctant to come here. So we decided to establish our own scheme and try and train our own home-grown staff. This would mean they would be more likely to stay and I guess more importantly they would be aware of the issues we face and buy in more easily to what we are trying to achieve especially for our more disadvantaged pupils. It's about making sure we have the right staff, if they're starting out with us, they quickly become aware of the culture we're trying to establish and what we want to achieve for children. We've had issues associated with recruiting sufficient good staff and with particular subject specialisms. By running our own scheme, albeit with support from the university, we hope to overcome those issues and establish a pipeline that will benefit all the schools involved. One other benefit has been the impact it's had on some of our existing teachers who have been reinvigorated by working with trainee teachers. We've always been strong on staff development, but this has moved things up a level. It's still early days but so far, it's been really positive, and we feel we are making progress on what has been a major problem for us.

In both Case examples, there was a desire to solve the problem of staff shortages, which are often faced by schools working in deprived areas, through growing their own staff. In these schools there was a recognition of the importance of establishing a culture and providing a training programme that reflected the demands of working in their schools. Training your own staff can be a useful way of addressing staff shortages, provided trainees are properly supported and given the opportunity to gain a broad range of experience. It is useful to make sure new staff adopt the teaching and learning approaches employed in the school, but they should also have the capacity to be creative and to have a range of teaching and learning methods at their disposal.

At the beginning of the chapter we considered some of the wider issues impacting on the training of teachers. Whilst recognising the problems of policy borrowing from other countries, it is worth looking briefly at one of the countries which is considered to have a very positive record in closing the attainment gap, Finland. Earlier in the book, we used the example of Finland and other Scandinavian countries to illustrate some of the social and economic policies that could be implemented to reduce social inequalities. In terms of teacher training and indeed broader staff development, Finland has been recognised as having a highly trained and skilled workforce (Sahlberg, 2009). There is a strong drive 'to educate all children in a system characterised by teaching excellence, and schools which are committed to collective responsibility for all children's, working with and supporting a climate of trust between educators and the community' (Abbott, et al., 2019: 81).

Thus, in such countries, there is no need to place special emphasis on teaching for children from disadvantaged contexts, because the focus is on *all* children. Does this suggest there are certain key principles in teaching and learning which can be applied to all children, whatever their context? Can staff be trained to understand and deliver these?

Continuous Professional Development

In the previous section, we considered some of the issues surrounding the recruitment and retention of teaching in schools in disadvantaged areas with large numbers of students from deprived backgrounds. We will now turn to the issues associated with existing staff and the strategies that can be employed to promote continuous professional development for all staff. It is important to remember an approach that we have constantly referred to due throughout this book – the significance of ensuring all staff, teaching and support, are included in any staff development programme. We would argue that a number of basic principles should underpin any staff development programme, particularly in schools working with significant numbers of disadvantaged students. Schools should:

- focus their energies and activities on learning, recognising that learning may come in many different forms as appropriate to a wide range of learners
- strike a balance between personal professional development and development which is for school benefit, ideally combining the two all the time
- establish and develop an ethos and ethic of enquiry
- recognise that learning can come from many sources – not just from formal teaching; external networks and stakeholders such as parents also contribute to learning
- accept that learning is a lifelong process and that the organisation's role is in making a contribution to this process
- focus on learning that will contribute to closing the attainment gap and will benefit a range of students, but especially those from disadvantaged backgrounds
- be in a continuous transformational state

(Adapted from Middlewoood and Abbott, 2015: 7)

For many schools, the drive to improve and to do things in a better way through challenging the status quo will be daunting, given other pressures such as staff shortages, lack of resources and political pressure the school might be facing. However, failure to undertake this process will result in even greater problems. Research carried out by Abbott and Bush (2013: 598) into outstanding primary schools in England has claimed that 'there was a strong emphasis on mentoring and coaching' and 'individual professional development was strongly supported' with 'a clear vision, accepted by all the participants, around improving the life chances of the children who attend the school'. Establishing a clear set of values around the importance of improving the life chances of the most deprived students with a clear goal of closing the attainment gap is a necessity for any school or college that is looking to be innovative and seeking to become a learning organisation. Undertaking

Research into Innovation in Schools, McCharen et al. (2011: 689) reported that 'a sense of shared purpose is a notable aspect of a learning organisation' grounded in 'shared commitments to values, such as the integrity of teaching or the need for social justice'.

Case Example 9.4

Judith is the head teacher of a primary school that has built its CPD programme around the idea of promoting social justice, with the aim of ensuring all students have the same opportunities despite differences in background and socio-economic status. She outlines her beliefs and what drives her vision for CPD in the school:

Let's be clear – I'm passionate about social justice, it's why I personally came into teaching and why I work here. There's so much wrong in society and this is such a deprived area and there's so much to do. I know I cannot change the world, but I can influence my little bit of it. So, whoever comes here, teachers, support staff, parents, pupils they all know what we are about. I need to be sure my staff are on board and I hope my enthusiasm rubs off, but I recognise that is not enough on its own. We have to create the right conditions and a really important part of that is to ensure the staff are given every opportunity to develop their skills. Our staff development programme obviously has raising pupil attainment at its heart. We have aspirations for all and that really underpins what we are about. It's important to get the right staff but we want to then give them the best chance to succeed. There are formal procedures including mentoring for all staff, lesson observations formal training inputs. However, it's important to learn from others. I'm a great believer in talking, so we provide structured opportunities for staff to share ideas and approaches. It's not just restricted to senior leadership or teaching staff; we involve everyone in different ways and at different times. I also like to involve staff in decision making, I suppose you'd say delegated leadership, but I want them to be aware of their actions and how it can have consequences. We support them as far as we can, given our budget, to attend outside events to get access to the widest range of ideas and approaches and we've had a small number doing MA courses. Underpinning it is a drive to get them to reflect on what they're doing, to think and to care. It's easy to get caught up in the day-to-day madness sometimes and it's important to be able to step back and think about what you are doing from time to time. I know some staff who were sceptical about being encouraged to take time to reflect. I'm sure they've seen the benefits in terms of improved practice. They need to care about their own professional development because they will then be able to do the best possible job for the children. It's important to remember that all this professional development has to have a focus and has to bring about real improvement for the children we are working with. It's great for individuals if it gives them the chance to progress but it has helped us give every child the best possible chance to succeed.

The head teacher in Case example 9.4 has a firm belief in her mission to reduce social inequalities for her students through the work the school does in the classroom and in the right community. She recognises the importance of staff development but understands it has to have a clear focus and purpose and resonate with what the school is trying to achieve. There is also a recognition that there has to be formal training and development, indeed this is essential to ensure high standards, but there is also the need to encourage and enable reflection on practice to take place in a supportive and positive environment.

Practitioner Research

As we outlined in Chapter 6, many of the schools we have visited and worked with in different countries had an emphasis on needs identification and support through in-house inquiry. We have been involved in a number of projects involving in-house inquiry and we have written extensively on this topic, see for example Middlewood and Abbott (2012 and 2015). In this section we will focus on practitioner research, which is research carried out internally by practitioners into the factors that enable effective teaching and learning to take place. It is often classroom-based, although it could also involve research into some whole-school issue. On a micro level, an example could be researching into the teaching of mathematical contexts with a specific class. On a macro level, it could involve research into the methods used to teach mathematics across a year group or across a whole school. It would involve staff investigating their own practice and attempting to develop strategies for improvement. Whilst accepting that this approach has limitations, for many schools and teachers this is an attractive form of research because it is rooted in their own practice and can lead to improvements in the classroom and in school-wide policy and practice. There may be other forms of internal evaluation that a school might carry out (e.g. organisational self-evaluation which will also relate to the type of external evaluation found in many countries), but in this section we will focus on practitioner research because we argue: 'the successful development of widespread practitioner research leading to a strong research-based professional learning community has tremendous potential. Not only can it fulfil the potential of all those involved as individual and collaborative learners, but this itself means that the school or colleges will be significantly placed to deliver real change, because it is based on what they exist for – the constant learning of those involved' (Middlewood and Abbott, 2015: 27).

We provide two Case examples of how practitioner research operates in practice and the potential benefits it can bring to schools, staff and students. However, we need to provide guidance on some underlying principles that underpin any practitioner research in schools aiming to reduce the attainment. Schools should:

- be honest and use an ethically based approach throughout
- have a clearly stated purpose which relates to improving the educational outcomes of disadvantaged students

- use the research instruments that are appropriate for the stated purpose
- analyse the objectives objectively
- come to conclusions based on actual findings
- make recommendations that are realistic and practical and based on the actual findings
- recognise the limitations of the research
- enable the researcher(s) to learn from the process and do even better next time

  (Adapted from Middlewood and Abbott, 2015: 29)

Case Example 9.5

Our first example centres on attempts to improve classroom practice in a primary school in a deprived area in the West Midlands of England. The research focused on getting nine-year-olds more interested in books and reading, especially those from households where there were no books at home and no history of reading. The teacher, Molly, got a small group of children to devise a simple questionnaire using short responses and tick boxes to find out what sort of books the other children in the class might be interested in and what the barriers were that prevented them from reading at home. Molly explained what this small-scale piece of research provided:

'We're constantly being encouraged to reflect and think about what we are doing and how we do. The head is always going on about it and making sure we can improve what we do. I'm lucky to be in a school that sees research as a strong part of professional development. I suppose it confirmed what I had always thought but it gave me ideas on how to try and develop a greater love of reading for my class. Problems at home which militated against the children reading included lack of a quiet space, boring books. Lack of time due to caring responsibilities for siblings and parents, and a feeling of it being uncool with family were all put forward by the children. As a response it made me look at the type of reading material, we have available. We've now got a much broader range and I suppose less teacher dominated. We have developed better communication with parents and tried to get them on board and we've given greater time and emphasis at school. I now run a lunchtime and after-school reading club. Nothing dramatic, it made me look at what we were doing with a fresh perspective. I suppose it has made a difference and the children really feel more involved.'

A second example is a rural secondary school in South Africa. The school had identified that a significant number of students, especially girls, were dropping out of the system after having a positive record of attendance at primary school. The school decided to investigate the reasons why there was a drop-off in the numbers of girls attending school. A number of reasons had been put forward, but the school required evidence to be able to develop a strategy to combat the problem. The deputy head teacher and the school administrator decided to go out into the primary schools and carry out some semi-structured interviews with primary school teachers and focus group interviews with final year students and with their parents. Vhonani commented:

'This was a big thing for us, and it took a bit of persuasion to get everything to fall into place. My head teacher was very supportive and he encouraged me to work with our administrator who will be involved in making sure we have the resources available to put policies into action. Well, it was just interesting going out visiting and speaking to people, we'd never really done it before. The schools are scattered over a large rural area and we have some contact, but nothing really properly formalised. I struggled to keep the interviews focused, they wanted to talk about lots of things, but I had a clear reason and I managed to mainly stick to it. There were lots of things that came out such as cost, problems with the provision of sanitary materials, the necessity to work at home to help with income, some views that girls did not need an education beyond the primary school.

There was also an issue about distance; we have students who walk miles to school each day, but there was also the added fear of safety for girls. Many girls and parents were worried about being attacked by men on the walk to school and back. In a sense there was nothing new about what they were saying but it gave us some information to try to develop a strategy. Obviously, we and the primary schools needed to communicate more clearly the benefits of secondary education and the opportunities it could provide. We also thought about transport and how we could help out. We now provide some bus transport but it's not really the answer and it's expensive and difficult to organise. So we decided to build a hostel, where we could put up those students with the furthest to travel. The parents and students were very keen on this. It sounds simple and obvious, but you can imagine the resource implications of doing this. We've had a lot of charitable support and although it's a poor area we have seen a real community enterprise develop. What started as a simple piece of information gathering has turned into a really big thing, but those visits provided the catalyst for the whole thing.'

These are two very different examples in terms of scale, but both are founded on the desire to improve the education of children from deprived backgrounds. In both cases, there was a clear focus and the research led to changes in practice and provision. However, neither project would have happened without the support of school leadership recognising the importance of enabling staff to undertake practitioner research to provide solutions to real-world problems.

In any teacher or member of staff, a commitment to professional development is an indication of a desire to improve and a willingness to change. This is an absolute prerequisite for success for anyone who works with disadvantaged learners.

Conclusion

To address issues of social inequality and the relative underperformance of certain groups of students, it is essential to have highly skilled staff who are able to work in a creative and effective manner. It is essential that all staff are given the proper levels of initial training to ensure they are the aware of the issues they are likely to face. They need to have been given the right skills to work in what can be challenging environments. As they progress through their career all staff have to be given appropriate further training and support to enable them to become even more highly skilled members of staff. As learning organisations, schools and colleges have to have a strong commitment to staff training and development. Without this commitment, it will be even more difficult to close the attainment gap.

In this chapter we have:

- discussed the role played by initial teacher training in preparing staff to work effectively with students from disadvantaged backgrounds
- considered the use of CPD to develop strategies to improve opportunities for disadvantaged students
- explored the use of practitioner research as a means to contribute to the reduction of the attainment gap

Chapter 10
Community Involvement

Introduction

Having noted earlier in Chapter 8 that collaboration between people is key to developments in raising achievement for those in disadvantaged contexts, this chapter widens this concept in considering how the most effective schools involve *all* members of the community in their and its development. The chapter therefore:

- argues that the school itself must be a true community in which all people, including learners, have a voice
- recognises that parents and family members are the most immediate link between school and the local community and therefore presents ideas for developments in this field based on successful practice
- suggests that the interaction between school and community is a two-way process and this concept is explored here
- refers to some of the barriers to such developments, especially for disadvantaged families
- finally, notes ways in which successful schools have overcome such barriers to achieve real community involvement

The School as a Community

The first requirement for any school, regardless of its setting, to be considered as working effectively in and with the community is that it should itself be – and be seen as – a community. Our research showed that school leaders everywhere who had been effective in raising achievement for learners from disadvantaged contexts believed in and tried to practise this notion. As one school leader in Plymouth, a city in the west of England expressed it:

> We cannot expect the future citizens in our societies and communities to want to be a part of them and a contributor to them, if they have just spent about a decade in an institution which is top-down led and very hierarchical, and where one group of people is seen as essentially superior to another. They will simply want to be part of that superior group when they are adults.

This school leader was referring, of course, to schools which operate on the traditional – indeed old-fashioned – model of the two cultures, that is one for staff and one for learners. Whilst few advocate complete equality for adults and children in a learning place, the successful leaders were clear that the days of the teacher being the fount of all knowledge to be passed on to learners were long gone. Just as important as the change in the traditional teacher/learner model, however, was the concept of everyone with a legitimate interest in the school having a right to and a responsibility for being an integral part of the school community. For the purposes of this section, we focus first on the importance of the learners' involvement, primarily by what is known as 'learner voice,' sometimes known as 'student voice' or 'pupil voice', depending on country or age of the learner.

Learner Voice

Internationally, with a few exceptions, learners in the twentieth century had remained in a state of 'traditional powerlessness' (Lumby, 2001: 7), but since then the move towards recognising the importance of learner voice has grown considerably, so that most – but not all – of the schools in our research had committed themselves to this practice and either had it well embedded in their daily lives, or were progressing in that way. In some countries, especially perhaps the Nordic nations, learner voice is a well-established element of the educational system, with students having access to government ministers, as a part of what Mortimore (2013: 206) describes as 'one of the ways in which the next generation of citizens is introduced to democracy'. Here, we are particularly interested in how it affects disadvantaged learners, and Flutter and Ruddock (2004) suggested that learner voice might help such learners understand that they have a legitimate place in the school community, whilst Ruddock and McIntyre (2007) proposed its beneficial impact on their self-esteem. It could be argued that school leaders have a moral responsibility to such students to involve them in the practice to help to avoid disillusionment and even possible denigration by established persons in communities and societies. The school leaders in our research were very aware of the dangers of token or pseudo democracy in offering learners a voice, and some research on school councils (Burnitt and Gunter, 2013) has found significant limitations to what these councils were 'allowed' to be involved in. Even in those countries where learner voice is actually written into the constitution, such as the Republic of South Africa, there can be no guarantee of success unless school leaders are committed and have support in promulgating it (Abbott and Middlewood, 2015).

In researching outstanding schools which had used the Pupil Premium Money effectively, according to official reports, Abbott et al. (2015) found that some school leaders had wanted to ensure that a certain number of such students were able to be representatives of other learners. Other leaders believed a way of assessing their progress in this field was to ascertain whether the number of such representatives increased over time. Thus, a deputy head in charge of a school council noted, 'Obviously, we want it to be just normal, as to whether a rep is a PP (Pupil Premium) student or not. When we don't notice it, it's worked!'

In these outstanding schools, all of which were in very deprived areas of a major city in England, focus groups of students were interviewed. Over 80 per cent of the children in the school were from very disadvantaged homes, and school staff ensured that this was carefully reflected in the composition of each focus group. The researchers found no distinction in any case between any particular type of student in their views on the value of student representation. The great majority of students had strong views on the importance of 'having a voice', and made no references to any distinctions between different contexts from which individuals came. There was one exception to this when a 14-year-old boy, Tony, said:

> It doesn't seem to matter who you are, it looks like we all want the same things. Douglas there, he won't mind me saying, comes from a much posher home than me. But we are pretty good mates really, and although we don't mix much outside of school, we think pretty much the same about this place.

Douglas in fact did not mind, said so and agreed with Tony! Discussion with staff afterwards found they were in the same subject sets and were expected to gain probably similar high grades in a year's time. The teacher who told the researcher this also said that Tony had been quite withdrawn in his first year at this secondary school, and felt that his election as a student representative and his subsequent experience had greatly increased his self-confidence and especially his ability to express his strongly held views on social justice.

It is important to note that in these schools, when a student proposal was rejected by staff as impractical, those adults were obliged to come to a meeting and explain carefully why the proposal had to be turned down. These debates were apparently 'fierce and fair' and usually ended in either compromise or understanding. As one girl student said, 'You realise that some of what you think are stupid rules (well, some are!), well lots are there for your own benefit and you hadn't thought about it that way before. I even explained some of that to my parents! My Dad had thought school was all about daft rules!'

Staff Culture

The second internal group of people integral to the development of the school as a community is those who are employed there, the staff. Whilst we say 'employed', we should note – and it is especially important in this community context – that this also includes anyone working on a voluntary basis in the school. The culture within which everyone works is the key to success in developing a sense of community in the workplace. Whether people are working there on a full-time, part-time, permanent or temporary basis, and whatever their role is, effective schools are those that share the same values and attitudes, even where they differ as individuals sometimes over how such things are practised. Here we describe some of the key features of and the principles that seemed to underpin the staff culture of these schools, based on what was seen on visits and what was suggested by staff personnel in interviews.

Concern for Everyone as an Individual

All the successful schools seemed to want to ensure that each individual member of staff, whatever their role, was treated as an individual, was valued as such and supported where necessary as such. We constantly heard expressions to the effect that, 'we all matter' or 'everyone matters here'. Common sense perhaps indicates that no school can care about each individual student or pupil if they do not demonstrate to colleagues that they care about each other individually as well. As one principal in a secondary school in Auckland, New Zealand, noted:

> We are all people first and teachers (or other staff) second, so we all have individual failings and weaknesses, however professionally we act. If we all recognise this, as we try to do in this school, I think, we'll do well by the students-who after all are the same. It doesn't mean we all have to like each other equally – that would be silly, as human beings will always have their likes and dislikes, but we all respect each other and try to understand that if we are all about the same thing – the students' welfare and progress – then we can all trust each other and become a real team.

Many writers, including ourselves (Middlewood and Abbott, 2017, pp. 22–25) have stressed the importance of diversity in developing a positive staff culture. Whilst such references to diversity normally refer, rightly, to the range of gender, ethnicity, age and experience, ability/disability, sexual orientation, religion and so on, here we also noted the diversity of personalities that seemed to exist across the range of adult staff. When we discussed this in one primary academy in Wales, where this had seemed particularly noticeable, the principal said:

> I totally agree. I think it took me a little while to realise that the children didn't want-and shouldn't have – lots of staff like me! Just as children are different, so staff need to be. When we select and appoint a new person, we now try to take that into account, although it is not always easy. It can't be an official criterion for selection, but when you are finally looking at the best 'fit' for the school, we certainly try to maintain a mix of characters. What a bore it would be if all the people who worked here – or in any school, come to that – were all the same! Terrible preparation for after-school life too, by the way!

When challenged as to whether there was a risk of inconsistency in behaviour within the school, the same principal's answer was, 'Of course! Frankly, I don't care if people behave differently from each other as long as three things apply – one, obviously they must be within the law and so on, two, the most crucial – they act in the very best interests of the child, and three, that we all remain committed to our own learning from every situation as we need to all be learners.' She added, 'Though I am reluctant to say this, I am the ultimate arbiter on what behaviour may or not be acceptable!'

Not all leaders took this stance, but each successful school allowed considerable freedom for individual staff to interpret the school's key values in action in different ways, as long as the child's interests were central. Here, 'interests' may be seen as a focus on the child's learning and aiming to constantly do better.

Equity and Openness

These successful schools were all fiercely committed to a sense of fairness and equity, which obviously fits with the notion of everyone being an individual to be respected. Staff tended to say that they had been treated fairly, even where they had disagreed with a decision. As Middlewood and Abbott (2017, p. 21) suggested, 'Perhaps the ultimate criterion for a school with an ethically based approach to its people lies in the situations that are unpleasant and when staff are inclined to say, "I do not like this at all, but it *is* fair."' In schools with a high proportion of disadvantaged learners, emotions can run high at times, so underlying principles of equity became important. It was also noticeable in certain schools that there was an openly stated approach to apologising. In one school in London, a notice on the staffroom notice board and in the staff handbook stated, 'Apologising is a sign of strength not of weakness. If you know or even feel you are in the wrong, say so and say sorry! And even if you are not in the wrong, if your rightful action has upset someone else, is there a place for saying sorry there too?' Such beliefs underpin strikingly powerful staff cultures and have a huge impact on the way school staff interact with others, such as learners and parents and visitors.

Emotional Health and Well-Being

As noted, these schools are often emotionally highly charged at times, as staff encounter challenging learners and parents, sometimes placing great stress on the employees. These successful schools seemed very aware of this and had learned to pay attention to staff's emotional health. Not only did some of them arrange for sessions on stress management, but they were sympathetic to personal crises in people's lives. Some of them had at least one senior staff member who was specifically trained in 'de-stressing' and staff were encouraged to notify that person if they detected any signs of potential stress triggers in a colleague's behaviour. Other schools had informal 'unwinding' sessions after the school day, where colleagues could chat informally about the day's tensions. In one school, the deputy principal said he knew it was known as the 'Whine shop'(!), but felt it was so much better than 'taking it home'. Humorously he added, 'Now, openly, I can hear someone say that they've had a tough day and they are going to the w(h)ine shop, and I don't now panic!'

It is likely that the understanding that leaders and senior staff recognised the pressures and stress that could be involved in their mutual work and tried to do something to help was a major contributory factor to the staff's willingness to commit themselves so completely to their work. Staff morale seemed extremely positive in these schools, with staff at all levels being highly motivated.

Parents and Family Members

Of all the members of a community who are external to the school, in that they are not obliged to be there on a daily basis, the parents and other family members of the students are clearly those who need to be most closely involved. Their importance has long been recognised in research into effective schooling, and the excellent schools we visited in disadvantaged and socially deprived areas had all made their involvement a priority.

In Part One of this book, we noted how a number of parents and whole families were indifferent and even hostile to becoming involved in their children's schools, primarily because of their own negative personal experience when they were attending school. Most of the successful schools recognised this and knew that they had to work very hard to restore parental confidence in their school's ability and willingness to work for the benefit of their children. Helen, the principal of a secondary school in the English Midlands city of Coventry said:

> When I took up this post, I could hardly believe just how 'anti-school' some parents were. Some were openly saying: "We don't trust you!" Overcoming this took about three years, I'd say. It took hours of patience, listening, persuading, cajoling, and even pleading to get where we are now, where I think I can say most parents believe that we are trying to work *with* them – for their children's sake.

Helen's early experience was not uncommon and where there was no hostility from parents, other leaders told of resignation and apathy in that the school could not do much, given the context, so why should they bother?

For some, however, the picture had not been all negative and several leaders told of how some parents were incredibly positive, however deprived the circumstances might be. Some, according to Sadiq, a deputy head in a London borough primary school, were 'desperately keen for their children to succeed at school so that they could have opportunities which had been denied to them'.

There are some extra key elements that seemed to be at the heart of what successful schools had done to gain parental involvement. This is not to say that the normal ways in which parents are encouraged to be involved were not used, because they definitely were. These include parents' evenings, open days, curriculum sessions, parents' rooms, parents' libraries, drop-in parent meetings and so on. These were widely and effectively used. What is worth noting are two additional factors which seemed important.

The first of these was to listen to the parents about what they thought was needed. Whilst this may sound obvious, in some circumstances such as described above, one of suspicion at the very least, more than one school had found this to be revolutionary. Sarah, a principal of a secondary school in a city in eastern England (the same one where Karen worked, whose story we related In Chapter 3), is talking about her experience in her previous school where she had been a deputy:

the first time I asked a parent what she thought her child needed and that I really valued her opinion, she (the mother) nearly fell off her chair! She had been so used to the school being the 'know-all' expert that she could not believe I wanted to know and certainly that I would do anything about what she might say. Overall, with her, and with the other parents, we tried to get them to see that, yes, we are the experts in our area –teaching and learning and related professional matters – *but* they (parents) had care of their children for a longer time than we did. We all knew the figures about how many hours children spent at school compared with home etc, as well as before coming to school and after leaving school! So we tried to get across that whatever picture they had of their own sons and daughters, it was genuinely part of the whole picture, which, put together with ours (the school's), could be the whole person –good and bad – which together we could all help to develop their full potential. Of course, it didn't mean you accepted everything parents said, but it did mean they had a perspective that was valid, just as the school's was. From there, we could together build on the positives and at school we could use aspects of parental 'expertise' to build better relationships with some students. For example, there were umpteen occasions when staff found out from parents about an interest that a student had that we had not known about, which staff used to get to know the student better or even build on in a specific subject area.

One might describe this approach, seen in most of the successful schools, as being akin to Wolfendale's (1996) perception of parents as:

- co-operating partners in the educational enterprise, and
- people whose expertise is equivalent and complementary to that of professionals

It is a bold step for a school to take to begin to think of parents as partners, when it is perhaps battling with parents and families who live in difficult circumstances and see the school as either alien or irrelevant. All the leaders who had set out on this path had found it difficult initially, but felt the rewards were enormous –for all parties concerned.

The second additional factor was to offer opportunities for parents and children to learn together. For parents of young children, such initiatives often involved various 'reading together' projects. In some schools, where a need had been recognised, these were 'Reading with Dad' schemes, including two different primary schools where children visiting a divorced or separated father at weekends could share specific reading tasks with him (with the consent of the other parent of course). As noted earlier, children's literature is continually being updated to provide content appropriate for the many different situations in which modern families operate. Sensitivity had been required in several cases where parental illiteracy was known to exist and this is referred to in the next section. Case example 10.1 illustrates how one school got families fully immersed in learning together.

Case Example 10.1

In a primary school in a large university town in the East Midlands of England, Vicky had been appointed about four years prior to being interviewed for this research. She said that she had made parental engagement a 'huge priority'. Despite the town having a famous university and being an attractive and popular place for visitors from all over the world, it has one neighbourhood with a history of poor housing, low-level crime, and general neglect. Vicky felt the resentment of her children's parents that when they mentioned the town to anyone, people assumed all was well. Her story was this:

'After a year of finding my feet, moving on a few unsatisfactory staff, and realising that working with the families and not preaching at them was the key, I appointed five staff members to be home–school visitors. Four were support staff who lived in the locality, and one was a teacher. They worked their socks off! They visited every home of a non-attender or reluctant attender, as well as many others. They drank innumerable cups of tea and coffee in people's homes! They spent masses of time listening to parental stories of hardship, complaint, mostly nothing to do with the school. They have a massive understanding of the neighbourhood community, the family feuds, the shortages, the gossip, and there is one important "rule". They promise not to tell the school any of what they are told, except where permission has been given, or when it is directly about the pupil concerned. That was crucial in the early days and trust was established. They were listeners first and foremost – and still are. We now visit every single family which has a child due to come to school for the first time – even if they have already another child already there.

Out of that work, we have established all kinds of facilities at the school – such as a quiet room for mothers to just come in, sit and chat (no school staff allowed!), a library for parents and children to take out books together – the return rate of books now is 99 per cent, whereas it was 50 per cent at first! We have a 'calming' area, where emotionally charged parents and/or children can come and let off steam before saying what might be regretted! These are all ideas which came from families, by the way. If a family gets into difficulties, I think we feel they could share this with the school. *But*, underpinning it all, so it is not "just tea and sympathy", it is making the parents believe two things – one, that their child or children *can* do well at school and, two, that they are not on their own – we can help. So, we have cases where parents are insisting their children attend school, that they do homework – it actually relieves teacher stress! The parents had so many ideas that the school couldn't keep pace, and so there are initiatives out there between parents that do not involve the school. For example, I know of one group of four families, where the parents do shift work, and night work, and they take turns to look after each other's children while the other parents are at work, making sure homework is done, for example. I know this, because they asked us for ideas for children's activities during the evenings!'

Other schemes encountered included ones in which parents and children worked together on projects such as a school vegetable garden (found in both a South African province and a central London neighbourhood). Further examples included where people were invited to learn a new skill, which both parents and children could learn together. (Computer development was popular because the children often knew more than the parents!) One school in an urban area, with a reputation for gang warfare and drug use, ran sessions on personal safety and self-defence which mothers and daughters attended together after school. Several schools organised cooking classes for parents and children to cook meals together.

Mutual Interaction between School and Community

The pioneering work in community services of people such as Dryfoos in the United States emphasised that the school was the 'most influential institution in our society' (Dryfoos et al., 2005: 9), and therefore services need to be focused there. However, it has also become clear that sometimes the school in the community is as important as the community in the school.

One of the features of those schools that were particularly successful in raising the achievements of disadvantaged and deprived children was that they were prepared to go out into the community and not rely on the members of the community coming to them. Given the negative and suspicious attitudes towards school held by many parents and families, this latter approach was unlikely to succeed, as several school leaders and staff recognised. One teacher in a school in Glasgow said, 'You don't break down barriers by sitting behind one of the barriers and waiting! You have to cross them and explore.' Thus, these schools adopted an approach that involved both welcoming people in and also sending people into the community. As described by Bella, an assistant head teacher in a London borough, the aim was eventually to achieve a situation where:

> parents, families and everyone else would see us as integral to the community so that the school becomes a place which offers certain things just like all the other agencies in the area – our main offering being learning and teaching of course. But we also want to be the place where suffering people or families can turn to us for some form of help. That will mean us being a conduit for other agencies of course, so we try to work closely with as many as possible.

Initiatives included:

- Enrichment activities which took the learners out of school and into the local community on visits to places such as art galleries, theatres, cinemas, sports venues, performance arenas, historic sites, bookshops and all manner of relatively simple places, such as local manufacturing sites, as well as disued airfields. As noted in earlier chapters, the absence of such activities can have a detrimental effect on children whose lives may be impoverished anyway.

- Visitors coming into the school – not only visiting or resident artists and writers, but also local business people, those willing to talk about their work in various fields, and those in public services such as the police or the fire service. Some schools asked pupils to vote for a 'local celebrity' who they would like to come into school, and the school would try its best to make this happen.

- Staff going into the community to share their skills – these included sports coaching, as well as some basic mathematics work with people who lacked confidence with numbers. Other 'subject areas' which included language skills and crafts of various kinds.

- To avoid any sense of appearing to patronise, some schools organised sessions in school where a parent or family member – or just a community member – ran events in which staff could participate as learners. Popular examples were seen in several schools with a high proportion of learners from ethnic minority backgrounds. One head of a food technology department in a secondary school in the multi-ethnic city of Leicester repor-ted: 'Obviously, I am reasonably expert at cooking, but I had a wonderful time in a class after school when a chef from a local Indian restaurant came in and showed us (parents and others) some fantastic new recipes! So, we repeated it with Chinese, and then Turkish chefs. I learned a lot!'

- Similarly, in a school in West London, a teacher of dance and movement had learned new movements and some specific Asian dances from group sessions led by an aunt of some pupils.

- Most of the above activities were found in urban areas, and, as noted earlier, schools in deprived rural areas may find it more difficult because of the distances involved, and the time taken for travel. Nevertheless, there were examples of community involvement, such as village elders coming into a primary school in a remote village in the northern area of Limpopo to talk about how local traditions and customs had originated. There were several examples of school and community collaborating over transport initiatives, and also of visits to farms, nature reserves and simply open spaces for obser-vation. One memorable visit involved learners and teachers being shown the importance of local rural crafts through an on-site workshop.

- Perhaps a quote from Bull (1989: 117) best summarises the aspiration of many of these schools: 'You wouldn't see the join between what the family was doing on the one hand and what the school was doing on the other. It wouldn't matter.'

Barriers to such Developments

All the leaders of all these successful schools agreed on one thing in particular – that it was not easy to achieve success! Without exception, they described what hard work it had been, especially in the early stages of the process. A few reflected on how they had felt like giving up in those stages, whilst others told of how they were the third or fourth school leader in a relatively short period of time – which strongly suggests that some previous leaders had indeed given up. More than one stressed the need for an 'unshakeable belief in what you are trying to do', while others referred to 'sheer stubbornness' on their part. At least three leaders made mention of not being prepared to settle for less than a hundred per cent, tempting though this was. Patrice, the principal of a school in Seychelles, expressed this thus:

> Having turned the school from a poor one to a pretty good one and been praised for it, it was tempting to think I'd done what could best be done. However, by that time, I was 'hooked' on improvement! I could not be satisfied until every single person in the school could be seen to be doing their best and achieving their potential. Those last few – perhaps 5 per cent of the students – were the toughest of all, and no one would have blamed me for writing them off. I am glad now I kept going and can be really proud, with all the staff, for what we've done.

If the amount of sheer hard work could be seen as a barrier of sorts, the other that was most frequently mentioned was the attitude of a certain number of school staff, especially what several leaders described as a 'hard core' of teachers whose attitude had to be overcome. These attitudes might be best expressed through comments such as:

> 'What else can you expect from children like these?'
> 'We do very well to get them to school at all, let alone get them to learn.'
> 'They don't stand a chance with their backgrounds.'
> 'We have to focus on those that want to learn.'
> 'You spend all your time on behaviour, so teaching is a secondary issue.'

As Chapter 9 showed, staff development lay at the centre of success in these schools. However, in most schools it had been necessary to remove a certain number of staff with the attitudes suggested above. This ranged from 'getting rid of' just a handful (two or three perhaps) of staff to a virtually wholesale 'clear out' as described by Paul, a primary school head teacher in the Midlands of England who said:

> When I was appointed head of this failing school, I interviewed every single staff member already there – there were 22 altogether. I told them what I was aiming for and told them they were either with me or not! Two were honest and said it couldn't be done and they would leave – which they did. I could at least respect their honesty. Three others took early retirement. About six were enthusiastic and turned out to be great colleagues, the rest had to go! I have been able to replace those with younger teachers who see the future as I do and they are wonderful to

work with. I am not necessarily blaming those others – it was the way things had been expected – but the children always come first.

In a few cases, this barrier was closely linked with an attitude among staff that regarded extended use of support staff or greater use of parents and community members as an undermining of their professional status, operating a kind of protectionism. On closer questioning, it appeared that teachers holding such views tended also to have the attitudes discussed above. Younger teachers, it seemed, despite their recently acquired professional status, tended to be more receptive to non-professional help and support.

Community Transformation

Some of the leaders, and indeed some of the other staff concerned, went further than any of the initiatives described in this chapter and spoke about actual community transformation. This quotation from Monique, a principal of a secondary academy in a deprived multi-ethnic area in London, describes this ambition well:

> My vision – and it can't be completed in my career lifetime – is of a community where people on leaving school want to stay and live and work in this area, where nearly all the teachers, not just the support staff, live in this area, and where a decent proportion of the school staff went to school here in this area. I think we have made a start and there's quite a way to go. When people from this area see this place (school) as a natural hub, along with other places, and when those who leave school to go off to university want to come back here to live and work because there are opportunities here, then we'll be there perhaps. Also – perhaps even more – when those leaving school don't see it as the end and they are not expecting to come back, but see it just as a stage and popping into this place for whatever reason is a norm, well – that might be it!

The 'start' that Monique referred to included being involved in teacher apprenticeships so that people could train on the job in their community to gain full teacher status, and employing local graduates who had not obtained posts to come into school as 'learning mentors' to students who were in danger of underachieving. The school also practised extensive home visiting by specially trained support staff to work with families of non-attenders. That school, like a few others, could be seen by community members as somewhere you might go for a range of services, of which education, including adult education, was one. In Cornwall, in the south-west of England, and in Bedfordshire, a southern county of England, specific health services for children and young adults were sited on or adjacent to school premises, where routine health or medical enquiries as well as specific issues such as sexual advice, drug problems and self-harm or other mental health topics could be shared with health professionals in confidence. Case example 10.2 describes a situation that several schools may well be aiming at as a long-term vision and are at various stages on the way to achieving.

Case Example 10.2

Tom, the principal of this all-through school in a very deprived area of a large city in Scotland was inspired by a visit made to New Zealand in 2013–14 and experiencing the use of family group conferences (FGCs). These were based on Maori communities, where the onus is on what the family's strengths are and not what their problems might be. Todd (2007) argued that deficit models for improving the lot of disadvantaged people would not work, because they are inevitably short-term. In FGCs, what each family can bring to a group is valued, whatever their circumstances. Tom said:

'We have made a start and I wouldn't say we are there yet, but we have seen a big shift in attitudes since we started a group, or rather groups. By respecting what families tried to do, however much they failed, we have found their self-confidence has grown and so has their respect for what other families try to do and for what the school tries to do. Most of all, families are turning to each other for help, before agencies. Where does the school fit in? It is an agency and a family so if you come into the school, you see parents talking to each other, talking with various agencies, without school help. Some staff families are involved – why shouldn't they be? And – not one teacher does what used to be called "pastoral" work (except where a teacher has specifically asked to). Teachers concentrate on teaching which they have been specially trained for. All support for learners is done by community members who, after all, are mostly parents, brothers and sisters, grandparents and so on. We give them training of course. Some are paid, some are volunteers. Come back in ten years to see if the whole thing has changed the whole community!'

Such community practice fulfils the aims of many educationalists and community workers, in that it puts the person and the family at the centre of everything and tries to suggest a network of support when it is needed which, ideally, would be there through a lifetime.

Summary

This chapter has:

- argued that the school itself must be a community, with a learner voice and an appropriate staff culture
- examined ways in which successful schools have engaged parents and families in their school life

- suggested that interaction between school and community should be a two-way process
- noted a few barriers to community involvement found by school leaders
- finally, described the ambitions of some of these schools to be able to transform communities

Chapter 11
Applying the Principles: An Extended Case Study in the US
Roberto A. Pamas

The principles presented in the book thus far capture how to enhance the learning of underserved students in ways that narrowed achievement gaps. They further serve as a key analytical tool for understanding what successful leaders were doing and how they did it.

Despite many years of dedication and hard work from educators across the United States to improve academic outcomes for underserved students, the achievement gaps continue to exist, however, there are some outperforming schools that have made progress in closing these gaps. While there also exists literature to enhance the understanding of the achievement gaps, the gaps in knowledge stem from the fact that there is limited research of how outperforming schools build professional capacity, allocate resources and execute programmes. The political landscape has also introduced new initiatives to address the problem; consequently, public schools face the challenge to rapidly adapt to the implementation of such initiatives. Thus, this tumultuous period in public K–12 education calls for further inquiry as to how schools have met the challenge of narrowing the achievement gaps.

The purpose of this chapter is to examine promising practices of an outperforming school in the United States that have narrowed the achievement gaps. The school selected for the study is located in a large suburban school district composed of mainly small single-family housing. The school consists of 987 students in grades six, seven and eight with an 80 per cent minority population representing 35 countries, 12 different languages, 15 different dialects and 65 per cent of the students are on free and reduced-price lunch. The languages and dialects consist of Amharic, Bengali, Cambodian, Creole, French, German, Japanese, Korean, Lao, Russian, Serbo-Croat, Spanish, Swedish, Tagalog, Thai, Urdu, Vietnamese, Yoruba, Ga, Krio, Tigrinia and Twi. There are four administrators, including the principal, 101 instructional specialists and teachers, 4.5 guidance counsellors and two safety and security staff members. There are 245 students or 25 per cent English Language Learners (ELL); 110 students in the Advanced Academics programme; 171 students receiving Special Education Services (some of these students are counted more than once because they receive more than one service).

Research

The research design chosen for this study was a case study enhanced with a survey; consequently, the rich description came from interviews, observations and document reviews completed during the case study, while survey data were analysed with descriptive statistics, reliability scores and factor analysis. In addition, the vast amounts of data collected were used to evaluate and explain the findings and to draw conclusions and are organised and reported by the four principles in action.

School Leadership and Management: Vision and Culture

Establishing a vision for the school is one of the core practices essential to leadership that influences student achievement. Without a clear and focused vision, schools are more prone to maintaining status quo behaviours and achievement gaps remain unaddressed.

The first visible writing displayed on the wall of Success School, as one entered the building, is the school mission statement:

> Success Middle School is committed to the belief that our mission is to provide a quality educational program in a caring and nurturing environment for all students. We hold high expectations for their academic success by providing standards-based classrooms where students master essential learning, as well as develop and demonstrate skills. Ensuring that students learn to be responsible and productive citizens is a major part of the middle school focus. We foster opportunities for students to reach their fullest potential, appreciate cultural diversity, become life-long learners, and seize all educational advantages that will prepare them for the 21st century.

This mission statement is not only on the wall of the school but also on the mind of the principal and staff members of the school. When the principal and staff members were asked about the vision of the school, their answers collectively resonated with the words from the school mission statement. The mission statement is so important to this school that it is not only posted in the front lobby, but is also included in the principal's weekly communication to the teachers to 'remind us of who we are and why we are here', according to the principal. One staff member said that the vision of the school is to 'celebrate the diversity of all students'. Another staff member said, 'Every child can learn, and every child can achieve success. We don't accept "I can't", you have to do it.' After 12 years as principal of the studied school, the principal said that his vision for the school still remains the same; he wants all students to be successful, he wants all students to be held accountable for their learning, he wants all students to seize all opportunities to prepare them for the twenty-first century and to be productive citizens of the world, and he wants all students to be successful as young people. Furthermore, he wants to share the responsibilities of student academic success by providing students with the best teachers who understand the needs of adolescents, setting the tone of learning with high expectations for everyone and ensuring that the school provides programmes (e.g. math counts, step and dance team, Latino club, yearbook, etc), to tap into students' interests and desires. He wants to provide the students with a variety of activities so that they continue to want to come to school.

In addition to inspirational posters and displays of student successes, the walls of the halls are filled with 'Follow the Success School Way – Take the Pathway to Success' posters. Further inquiry revealed that the poster is part of the Positive Behavior Support (PBS) programme, which is a school-wide behaviour plan that required students to 'be prompt, be polite, be safe, be prepared, be productive'. According to the principal, student disciplinary issues have reduced by 50 per cent since the adoption of the Positive Behavior Support model a year ago; it is extremely important to 'have the teachers' cooperation' stated the principal. When asked about the discipline in the school, one staff member said, 'We don't have bad behaviours at Success School; rules are enforced here'.

In addition to the Positive Behavior Support programme, the school also implements a programme called 'Lockout' to encourage students to get to class on time. In this programme, teachers are instructed to lock their doors when the bell sounds. Students who are locked out would report to administrators positioned nearby in the hallway. Students who do not have a valid hall pass would be logged in to a database and parents would be called. If the same student is locked out a second time, the student would be required to attend Saturday school detention. This success was further evidenced by the fact that very little time was wasted between the changes of classes; students hurried to get to the next class on time, teachers were observed standing at their door greeting students as they entered, and administrators also stood in the hall. As one staff member confidently announced, 'If you turn the corner from here, you will see an administrator standing there'. She was right; an administrator was seen standing where the staff member said he would be. The principal also stationed himself in the hallway, talking to students and always calling them each by name. A similar procedure occurred at the end of the day; administrators and counsellors attended their designated posts inside the school and on the bus ramp. The feeling of a warm and caring culture was validated over and over again and evidenced by the interactions among the adults and students at the school. A counsellor was heard asking a student how her day was as she walked by him to the bus ramp.

While the school community itself is notably heterogeneous and diverse, many people at the school described its culture as being warm, friendly, nurturing and caring. The principal confirmed this culture and attributed its success to 'the commitment of everyone to meet the needs of the child in the middle. The school has implemented many innovative programmes, practices, and strategies to address the school's changing demographics and students with special needs.'

Continuing with the principle of leadership and management, how did the principal in this studied school see himself as an effective manager and, at the same time, embrace his responsibility for students who were underachieving? The principal wanted to ensure that teachers have the resources they need to teach, protect time for teaching, manage student discipline, and establish programmes to meet the needs of students. When asked if the principal provided enough resources for the staff, one staff member said, he will give us 'anything that we need for our programme as long as we can justify the needs'.

Many staff members appreciated the low student–teacher ratios and the latest in technology for student and teacher use, including at least six mobile carts with 15 laptops in each cart, four computer labs with about 25 computers in each lab and numerous smart boards with LCD projectors. As another staff member stated, 'The plethora of technology helps students to be successful and to quickly synthesise information'. The average class size is 25 students to one teacher; however, an elective teacher did say that one or two of her classes might have 30 students.

Moreover, staff members stressed that the low student–teacher ratio contributes to time on task. In addition to agreeing that the principal is supportive in providing teachers with whatever teaching resources they need and protected time for teaching, staff members also agree that the principal manages student discipline. As one staff member said, 'SR&R (Students Rights and Responsibilities) are drilled into the students' mind a lot'. Overall students appeared to be well behaved and well-mannered as they transitioned from one class to another; they also appeared to know what was expected of them in and out of the classroom. As the principal visited classrooms, he did not hesitate to stop and discipline the student as he saw fit, as he said to one student in a physical education class, 'Where is your uniform? You know better than coming to this class without your PE uniform? I don't want to see you without a PE uniform again. Have I made myself clear?' 'Yes, sir,' was the reply to the principal by this particular student.

When asked about the effectiveness of the principal as a programme manager at the school, one staff member said, 'The most important thing that the principal did for the teachers and students at this school was to create a climate for learning.' Another staff member summarised what she thinks about the principal:

> One thing that impressed me about this school is its cleanliness. In addition, there are a lot of technology and teachers help students to be successful. Teachers promote higher order thinking in teaching students; anything that helps students to be successful, Success School's teachers will help the students to do it. Teachers are also passionate and competitive. Instructional practices are based on analysis of data. Most importantly, these things would not be possible without the effective leadership of our principal.

Collaboration and Staff Development

In addition to the teaming concept and professional learning communities utilised by Success School, the principal relied heavily on his two instructional coaches and site council to help him with academic decisions impacting the teachers and students. Instructional coaches do not have classroom responsibilities but are on-site professional developers who worked with classroom teachers on research-based teaching strategies to improve student achievement. Instructional coaches meet weekly with administrators and department chairs to plan; they also worked one-on-one with teachers to make it easier to adopt the instructional strategies that can make a difference to students' success. These coaches meet with teachers individually at a convenient time for the teacher, either during a planning period or after school, to identify the teacher's needs and to discuss possible research-validated interventions that might help the teacher address those needs. Depending on the particular needs of the teacher and/or team, duties of these instructional coaches include observing classes, collaborating on interventions, preparing materials, modelling and providing feedback. According to the principal, these instructional coaches 'have been wonderful additions to his school and are instrumental in the positive changes in instruction in the classroom' and they worked in partnerships to accelerate teachers' professional learning through mutually enriching relationships.

The site council is an academic advisory committee consisting of team leaders, department chairs, counsellors and administrators. The council meets once per quarter, along with the administrative team, and makes academic decisions for the entire school. As the principal stated, 'I don't want to make decisions that impact the entire school without the input of the teachers.'

Furthermore, other academic decisions are also made at the daily team meetings where teachers and the administrator for that grade level discuss issues, problems and solutions. All teams used these meetings to discuss student progress and team-related activities. The administrator for that grade level is required to attend at least one meeting a week.

In addition to professional learning communities, site council and team meetings, the principal also depends on the teachers to revise and/or create a school plan every year. At the beginning of each school year, the school planning committee, composed of the same members of the site council and two parents, meet to write the annual school plan. The team studied the test data and determined the school's greatest academic needs and developed solutions and strategies to be incorporated into the school plan, which is due to the central office by 1 December each year. In order for the school plan to be successful, the principal stressed the inclusion of the following practices which have become a part of life for students, staff and community members of Success School:

- school-wide commitment to improving student achievement
- shared responsibility by all teachers
- continuous evaluation/curriculum mapping
- variety of instructional techniques
- direct standards-based instructions
- daily reading comprehension and writing strategies
- vocabulary development with a focus on standardised testing words
- common planning time
- library and media research
- infusion of technology
- intensive standardised test review with the use of education resources such as Buckle Down and Coach and a focus on the essential knowledge
- test-taking strategies and/or tips
- daily mental math skills

- standardised test review period and remediation
- extended learning day assistance
- international Baccalaureate assessments and research

Toward the end of the school year, around May or June, the same committee evaluates the school plan to see if benchmarks are met and what recommendations to make for the next year.

Another dimension of collaboration at the studied school is in the hiring process. The principal stated clearly that he wanted the team members to provide input into any vacancy in their team. The administrators interviewed the prospective candidates and then the teacher team conducted the second interview with the candidates forwarded to them by the administrators.

The team would then rank the candidates in their preferred order and the principal would make the final offer to the selected candidate. The only exception to this process would be during the summer months where it would be difficult to assemble the entire team of teachers; the principal then would 'invite any team member who might be around to join me in the interview'.

Family and Community Involvement

The location of the parent liaison's office is the best indication of how important family and community involvement is to the studied school and the principal. The office of the parent liaison is next to the principal's office. 'If she needs to update me about an issue relating to the community, then she would be able to do so immediately', said the principal when asked about the location of the parent liaison's office. The principal stressed the importance of the role of the parent liaison in his school. 'She is the bridge between the community and the school' he said; through phone calls and conferences, she made positive communication with parents and helped them to feel more self-confident, more comfortable with the school and more likely to become involved. The principal further described the parent liaison as the pulse of the community who updated him every week with special events and situations in the community. The parent liaison also admitted that she helps the principal 'to be more visible in the community through my voice and outreach'. He also stressed the importance of having a full-time parent liaison that is fluent in multiple languages instead of one who is part-time and might not be fully invested in the philosophy of the school.

In addition to the monthly scheduled parent teacher association (PTA) meeting, the studied school also hosted family outreach meetings where parents who might not have attended the PTA meeting could attend and learn important information and/or have any questions that they might have answered. Furthermore, the principal also used the PTA meetings to have workshops to help parents to understand school policies and procedures and to strengthen the relationship between the school and the community. The principal also pointed out the need for staff members to be part of the PTA by offering prizes for teachers joining the PTA.

Beside the focus on increasing the understanding and respect for student and family diversity and creating a more caring school climate, the principal also stressed the significance of celebrating diverse cultures. In February, the school completed a month-long celebration of African American History Month and the Reflections Program sponsored by the PTA to be followed by the annual family fitness night sponsored by the physical education department in April and the international night later in May.

Another form of outreach to the community is the flow of continuous communication from the teachers to parents. The teachers communicate with parents via conferences, newsletters and the use of the internet. Furthermore, the school also hosted a fall touch base program and a spring touch base program where parents have opportunities to dialogue with teachers before going to work since the school operated on a two-hour delayed opening on these two days. Undoubtedly, the principal and teachers at the studied school understand the importance of creating partnerships with the community to help students to succeed in school and in life.

According to a staff member, 'relationship is the key; kids need to know that you care about them. I attended their games and activities outside of the school setting. In addition, every student received a small gift from my team on their birthday.' When families are involved, according to the principal, students have common messages from home and school about the importance of attending school, staying in school and working hard. The principal ended his message in every newsletter with the statement, 'We recognize that parent involvement and participation is essential to your child's success in school. We appreciate your ongoing support.'

Making the Dream Real: Student-Focused

The study analysed has demonstrated that when educators believe that positive change can happen and leaders begin to systematically envision how it will, together they begin to turn schools around and lift all underserved students. Great leaders and educators know to place the needs of their students ahead of their own wishes; there is no other option if we are going to be successful in narrowing the academic gaps.

One success story shared with me by the principal and teachers at the studied school demonstrated the discussed principles of collaboration and family engagement. The studied school was particularly proud of and often celebrated the success of their weekly home visits. This was an idea introduced by the principal and slowly embraced by the administrative, school counselling and instructional staff. Based on the school's strong culture of collaboration between teacher teams and school counselling staff, the administration frequently received feedback that it was challenging to involve parents or family members of struggling students; these parents or guardians were not available for meetings with teachers or school support staff during regular school hours. While teachers believe that parents should be more involved, but seem at a loss as to how to make that happen when parents could not be available due to various circumstances; similarly, parents often feel disconnected from their child's teacher and the school. As a result, the idea of conducting home visits after school hours originated with a simple purpose of being able to meet with parents or guardians and communicate their child's behaviour and academic progress.

The purpose of this story is not to explore quantitative and/or qualitative effects of a single home visit on relationships between the teacher and parents, teacher–student relationships, student behaviour, work habits and academic achievement, but to provide anecdotal observation on the effectiveness of home visits as a practice at the studied school. Based on this understanding, the principal shared with me that structurally they, as the first school in their district, started this initiative by asking each grade level to identify about 15 (5 per cent) students for a total of 45 during the first year who needed this visit based on all available data. The plan for that first year was to conduct home visits once a week with the goal of meeting three families during the two-hour time frame. The original membership of the home visit team consisted of the principal, the assistant principal and school counsellor of the associated grade level. After the third week of the visits and based on positive feedback received from parents and students, grade-level teachers began to join the team, which added another meaningful and powerful dimension to the overall visit. The principal proudly shared as he continued with the story and with a big smile on his face, that the morning after the first night of the visit, as he was monitoring and greeting students in the cafeteria, students flocked to him and one by one asked if he and the team could visit their house the following week. Students had communicated and heard, within the time frame of 12 hours, that the school cares about them as individuals and their overall success. As previously articulated by one staff member, '. . . kids need to know that you care about them'; that initiative and that first night was the flame that ignited the intrinsic motivation within students to be successful. They believed that what they do matters to the school and its staff because they care. The communication occurred between the school and parents that night was so powerful and meaningful that it prevented 42 out of the 45 students (93 per cent) identified by their teachers from having to attend summer school that year to successfully move on to the next grade level.

This successful story was not intended to address effective models to show how teachers can develop the skills needed to make home visits more productive. It does, however, demonstrate the value of building positive relationships with parents and students and the power of collaboration and family engagement, since the rewards have consistently shown to be worth the effort. Undoubtedly, successful leaders and educators need to continue to focus on students' needs.

Whilst the above story illustrated the importance of focusing on students' needs to narrow achievement gaps, many teachers at the studied school also echoed the theme of support that they received from the principal and administrative team. As one staff member said, 'The most important thing that the principal did for the teachers and students at this school was to create a climate for learning'. When asked about this, the principal shared with me that he achieved this by keeping the focus on learning and it started with him making sure that teachers were clear on the school's vision and expectations for all staff members. He continued to share that remembering 'teachers don't know what they don't know', it is his job and that of all administrators to teach them. Successful leaders focus on students by focusing on the needs of their teachers. To this end, the principal stressed the importance of classroom observation and feedback to teachers as a strategy and practice to reinforce successful teaching practices and improve on mediocre skills. He modelled this behaviour for his assistant principals by making it a priority to visit a minimum of five classrooms every day, which was dotingly referred to as the principal's 'five-a-day.' I witnessed this activity when I visited the school one day, and his administrative assistant informed me that he was doing his 'five-a-day.' Furthermore, at the end of each visit, he and his administrators provided each teacher with feedback on what they observed and invited teachers to see them if they would like to discuss the observed lesson further. In addition to these observations and feedback, he also created a culture of collaboration by inviting teachers to observe each other to share effective strategies and practices. As he said with a smile, 'The best part of my day as a principal is visiting classrooms and observing learning by students and teaching by teachers'.

This studied school has faced challenging circumstances but has succeeded in increasing and sustaining achievement levels over time. It has successfully demonstrated that it is possible to break out of the cycle of low expectations and achievement. These stories of educational success focus on individual students, exceptional teachers and an exemplary school; however, it takes an excellent school leader to ensure successful school and culture for students, staff and community. By sharing these stories, I hope to provide some assistance to those who courageously take on the task of leading schools to ensure academic success not just to some but to all students, regardless of race or ethnicity, economic status, residence, native language or disabilities.

Summary

In the United States, prior to the implementation of the Every Student Succeeds Act (ESSA) in the 2017/18 academic year, education standards were largely determined by federal standards outlined in the No Child Left Behind Act (NCLB) of 2002. As a law, NCLB was intended to measure where students were making progress and where they needed additional support, regardless of race, income, zip code, disability, home language, or background. Over time, however, NCLB's prescriptive requirements became increasingly unworkable for schools and educators. As a result, it did very little to address the specific needs of the most disadvantaged communities, but further exposed achievement gaps among traditionally underserved students and their peers and impelled an important national dialogue on education improvement.

Consequently, the Every Student Succeeds Act (ESSA) strives to improve students' chances at Success by encouraging a more personalised approach to students' needs, interests and strengths as well as improving and decreasing the emphasis on standardised testing, which should advance individual state school system goals to better impact students' achievement. It should also advance equity by upholding critical protections for America's disadvantaged and high-need students.

While it is important for all of us, parents, teachers, leaders and community members, to work with policy makers to address factors contributing to the educational shortcomings in some of our schools and to equitably utilise all tools and resources available, it is equally important to transition from policy to application. Accordingly, the principles identified in this book confirmed practices that must be in place in order for leaders to influence learning outcomes to close the achievement gaps. Furthermore, successful practices identified and demonstrated represent the principles of school leadership and management, collaboration, staff development and family and community involvement. This study further reinforced the practices that leaders must continue in order to see measurable results in closing the achievement gaps. Consequently, leaders must:

- model to all staff members that the main priority of the school is the success of all students
- be knowledgeable about current practices of curriculum, instruction and assessment
- monitor the effectiveness of school practices and their impact on student learning
- know when to give teachers a clear voice in decisions that impact the academic achievement of students
- develop strategies to address the needs of non-English speaking families to encourage them to come to school and be active participants in their child's learning
- provide teachers with materials and professional development necessary for the successful execution of their jobs
- ensure that faculty and staff are aware of the most current theories and practices in education and make the discussion of these practices integral to the school's instructional culture

In addition to these promising practices, the study also identified areas for improvement on which leaders will need to focus:

- keeping the teacher–student ratio low
- allowing staff members to actively participate in the hiring process
- ensuring that the staff reflects the ethnic make-up of the student body

- encouraging parents to visit the school more frequently
- ensuring that the principal continues to visit classroom frequently
- establishing the school as a centre of the community
- encouraging members of civic or social organisations to volunteer in the school
- encouraging parents to participate in after-school programmes
- encouraging school staff members to hold classes for parents
- encouraging students to participate in extended year schedule

Final Thoughts

In this chapter, I wanted to capture, as much as possible, the voices of the principal and teachers because I believed that their experiences, behaviours and motivations are best described by them and their work. I also wanted to move beyond stating the existence and extent of achievement gaps to explain how Success School has addressed them.

While closing the achievement gaps is an extraordinary challenge, the successful implementation of promising practices from the studied school demonstrated that it is possible to change the educational experiences of previously underserved students in order for them to learn and perform at a level close or equal to those who have traditionally prospered in the US education system.

Universally, children begin life with different opportunities to achieve their goals; however, they come to schools with the hope of learning and growing in ways that will allow them to maximise their potential. Every day parents are sending their best children to schools, as I often reminded committed educators that they are not keeping their best at home, and entrusting their most important possessions to the educators; as a result, we, as educators, are obligated to do our part to teach all students to the best of our ability. As leaders, we are obligated to prepare our teachers to be the best educators that they can be. We need to do more than just continue to describe the problems confronting our schools, instead, we must never give up finding solutions to address these problems.

As I wrote this chapter, the world experienced a major crisis – the COVID-19 pandemic – which has changed the way we live, study, work and connect with each other. As education leaders navigate their communities through this crisis, it is important that they plan for what comes after; normalcy after this pandemic for students, families, teachers, leaders and community members will be changed. Students who experience daily trauma from poverty may have lived through even worse through the loss of friends or family due to coronavirus-induced illness or losing parents' income. As we transition from face to face to virtual learning, there are many questions for subsequent research, such as:

- What do students, families and teachers need most to make digital learning work? What are they most concerned about?

- With so much diversity in resources and capacity among families, how can digital learning system be designed to meet everyone's needs?

- How will this pandemic impact the existing academic achievement differences between middle-class and low-income students?

Ultimately, the most effective strategy to narrow the achievement gaps is for us to always remember that children come to school to learn, and it is a moral imperative for all educators to provide them with the most equitable opportunity to achieve their maximum academic potential. The time has come for us, committed educators and courageous leaders, to stop discussing and debating social justice, but actually to do the work of social justice so that we can become a beacon of hope for all children and school systems across the world.

Part Three

Conclusions and Proposals

Chapter 12
Conclusions and Proposals

Introduction

This final chapter draws on the data collected and collated in previous chapters. It reflects on the many Case examples we have shown of successful practice in this field. The chapter is essentially a practical one, containing relatively few references. When we explored the topic of the underachievement of disadvantaged learners, through researching the successful practices of many schools, their leaders and staffs, our aim was to see if it was possible to identify particular actions or approaches that might be used by those wishing to commit themselves to raising the achievement of such learners.

We believe we have been able to identify some, and this chapter sets them out. This is not out of any sense of presumption, but in the hope that the new inspirational leaders and teachers who are needed in these contexts will find them helpful. In effect, the chapter may seem like a list of things to do (plus a few don'ts!), supported by a few suggestions which a school leader might find appropriate in their specific situation. Every one of the suggestions and proposals is firmly based on something we have either observed or that has been described to us by someone involved in it. The chapter therefore:

- briefly suggests some key principles that those operating educational systems of different kinds might consider in adapting the system to narrow the achievement gap
- proposes specific actions that may help aspiring and current leaders of schools in disadvantaged contexts
- includes practical suggestions that have worked for some leaders
- suggests specific ideas for teachers and other staff to help them succeed in raising achievement for disadvantaged learners
- indicates how such actions may be applied to all those working or aspiring to work for success in this field

Educational Systems: Ideas/Principles for Change

As we have noted more than once already in this book, the COVID-19 pandemic has widened the attainment gap between poorer and more prosperous learners. In England, a report by the Education Policy Institute's (EPI) research found that the months of lost learning would compound disadvantage and undermine any levelling-up programmes. Two of the partners in the report went so far as to say: 'Without systemic change, this gap will never close' (Butters and Cicerone, 2020: 4). What are some of the systemic changes that are needed?

Throughout this book we have focused on practical initiatives employed by schools and colleges to close the education gap. These are likely to benefit individual institutions and particular students. Whilst being extremely useful on a micro level we also, need to consider some of the broader societal changes that need to take place, as well as some specific suggestions for change within the education system as a whole.

Earlier in the book we briefly considered the impact of a redistribution of income from the better-off parts of society to those who are more disadvantaged. This will not automatically lead to a reduction in the education gap, but it would create a fairer and more just society which would provide the basis to improve the life chances of the most disadvantaged. This would have a direct impact on some of the causes of educational disadvantage and would lead, for example, to improved housing and better health care. Allied to improved infrastructure and more employment opportunities in the most deprived areas, this policy is likely to have a profound on the causes of disadvantage. There has to be a concerted effort to reduce child poverty through a long-term strategy. This could be achieved through changes to the taxation system, social security and focused government expenditure.

As part of this strategy improvements should be made to early-years education and to enhanced childcare provision and parenting classes for new parents. Increased resources are only part of the solution. They have to be employed together with a drive to develop greater belief that education can make a difference, alongside increased parental involvement. There has to be much greater investment from parents and society more widely in the benefits of education, that it can really make a difference to a young person's life. Without this change in emphasis to a belief in the power of education, localised policies will only make marginal differences.

These wider changes in how society and the economy works must be reflected in the way in which education operates. We would advocate some key fundamental priorities for any education system:

- a proper level of funding across the system designed to improve facilities and provision

- additional funding for the most disadvantaged school and college students, especially in areas that have suffered long-term decline

- a strong emphasis on training and staff development to ensure a highly qualified and motivated workforce

- provision of resources to deal with the ongoing impact of the COVID-19 pandemic

- greater involvement of parents, the wider community and students in the education system

- an emphasis on academic excellence, with improved access to higher education

- equal status given to technical and vocational education

- recognition that education is about more than examination success

- less emphasis on selection, private education and elite institutions

We are realistic enough to accept that these changes can only come about through the political process and by consensus within society. However, it is our belief that they would benefit the whole of society, lead to a reduction in the social problems referred to earlier in the book and improve the life chances of all members of society. They would provide the basis for the creation of a fairer and more just society and enable real work to be undertaken to close the achievement gap.

As our research has found, even in the current context, with many of the above principles not existing in various systems, some schools are achieving remarkable things with children and young people from hugely disadvantaged backgrounds. We now suggest actions that various key people might consider, to achieve the same outcomes.

Aspiring School Leaders

There may be teachers reading this book who are not yet school principals or head teachers, but who have an ambition to become one. Such people are, of course, likely be careful in deciding where they apply for the leadership. If we were to pass on any advice from leaders we have met and interviewed as they drew on their own experience and that of others, it would include the following:

Do not apply for the leadership of a school in a hugely disadvantaged context with a poor record of achievement unless:

- you are completely committed to that kind of school and are determined to succeed there
- you are prepared to be 'in for the long haul', as one principal put it. She pointed out that there are 'no quick fixes although you may need some quick wins'. Other leaders pointed out that you can do more harm than good by arriving, achieving some immediate success and then leave for another post. One head teacher said bluntly: 'In my view, if a leader came here to notch a success on their CV before moving on, they would do children like these great harm. They need security and people they can respect. My strong advice to any leaders would be not to come to a school like that at all if you are not prepared to stay and do a complete overhaul over a period of years'
- you are willing to work very long hours and give yourself to the job pretty well all the time – even become exhausted at times
- you can deal with extreme stress and have a very thick skin
- you have a supportive home environment or network with people who will understand and share your commitment

Kevin, a principal of a highly successful secondary school in a deprived area of a Scottish industrial city, had this to say to people ready to seek their first leadership post:

Never say to yourself, 'I want a principalship and at any price!' Some jobs will not
be worth your health being ruined and then feeling a failure. Only go for this kind
of school if you really, really want to give your all for these young people and are
willing to make sacrifices! There are plenty of other posts where you could
probably do a good job for the students there. They also need good leaders and
deserve them – we must not forget them. Not everyone is cut out for this kind of
job – or is it just for odd people like me!

Preparing for the Job

Let us now imagine you have applied successfully for school leadership – what
practical steps might be taken before you actually start work at the school? Some of
the following advice might apply to any school, of course, but some of it is specific
to schools such as those dealt with in this book.

Be clear in your own mind about your ultimate vision for the school. What would
you hope the school would be like and in, say, five years? Visions of course have to
be rooted in reality, otherwise they remain unachievable. Your notion of the future
may have to be slightly amended as you discover more about things, but you do need
something to convey to others – the staff, the learners, the parents. If it is something
that others may see as unattainable initially, that does not matter; it will make its
achievement all the better.

What are the values on which this vision is based? You will know what your
values are, educationally, personally and societally. How will you know that your
values are being put into practice as you strive to attain this vision? Are these values
'demonstrable', as Davies (2006: 43) called them. You can even make a list for
yourself, as Georgina, a US vice-principal who emailed us on this topic, suggested.
She said she did it and, for example, included 'self-confidence and ability to take on
problems' as applied to staff. She said:

> I wrote down in my own personal diary that in about two years maximum, people
> would be bringing many fewer of their problems to me, because they would have
> learned to tackle these themselves, and the number of incidents recorded would be
> reduced. Staff would be telling me of incidents and saying that a percentage of
> these had already been dealt with. This for me would be a guide that they were
> gaining confidence in their ability to handle difficult situations. It was rough and
> ready as a measure, but it helped us all and I made sure I put in the support early
> on of course.

What kind of ethos would you hope to see established in the school as it improves?
Our evidence suggests it should, above all, be a collaborative one where nobody
feels they are on their own, and everyone comes to realise that working together is
what helps bring achievement for all. A sense of fairness, openness and transparency
are also likely to be key elements of this ethos.

Practical Suggestions:

Find out as much as you can about the area from which your children or students come, where they live and spend their time. As well as immersing themselves in the data about the area, housing, employment rates, and so on, several of the successful leaders we met said they had physically explored the area around the school to get a 'feel' for where there learners spent most of their time. It is one thing to know an area is 'disadvantaged', it may be quite another to see the actual streets, shops, cafes, workplaces and places of amusement and the conditions both of them and the people who run them. Leaders who had done this said they found it 'enlightening', as well as 'depressing'; as some pointed out, it was also very useful knowing the names of a few neighbourhoods, streets and shops because, when a learner referred to one, they were always surprised that the new principal had any idea of such things!

A small number of leaders had arranged to personally meet a range of the school's learners before the first term began. A particularly striking example came from Josie, as she started her first term at a school in the most deprived borough of a Midlands city in England. She described how:

> I got the deputy head to make a list of what he saw as the dozen worst students in the school from the previous year! Excluding a few who very rarely attended at all, I arranged for ten of them to have appointments with me on the first day; seeing them all separately took me about three hours altogether, but it was well worth it. Each one of them (seven boys, three girls), came in individually, each expecting a good telling off from the new boss! The first thing I told them was to sit down. They had only ever been in this room for disciplinary reasons. I sat opposite, not behind a desk, but this was no softly, softly session. My approach was to say that I had studied their files (which I had – in detail) and wanted to know why they were doing so poorly, when it was obvious to me that they were capable of being successful. Why did they think they were doing so badly? I listened to the usual excuses, blaming others, friends, teachers, families and then said the school was not going to allow such under-fulfilling of potential and what we were going to do was x or y. I used 'we' all the time – it was all about what 'we' were going to do. We then agreed first steps and off they went, with me saying 'We'll be checking on this tomorrow, next week or whatever.' Where I felt they had a genuine grouse (about a class arrangement, or a staff member for example), I promised to look into it and of course, I did so. Where there seemed to be an out-of-school issue, I noted it and had action taken as best I could. I pulled no punches and where relevant, I got them to agree they had been lazy, for example, and that was not acceptable for someone with their potential. Not only was all this good for those particular learners, but word spread like wildfire (staff as well!) and I know it was a huge help in all the other things I did that first year.

Being the Leader

If and when you do become the leader, principal or headteacher of a school in a greatly disadvantaged area, here are some of the key areas on which your success may well depend.

The Recruiting and Selection of Staff

Any success you get will depend upon the staff, so this is crucial! Of course, you will inherit staff and will satisfy yourself, probably by a series of individual meetings, which ones have the qualities and skills needed to work with you in achieving success. You may well do a staff audit through which you can assess as a whole whether you have, for example, sufficient diversity and whether this can reflect what is needed to meet the needs of this particular context. According to the successful leaders interviewed, diversity meant a range of:

- age and experience
- gender
- ethnicity
- personality

However, when new staff are appointed, you will have the all-important opportunity to create even greater staff cohesion and ensure a totally focused and single-minded staff to ensure success for the particular learners. We asked leaders to name the key qualities they needed in teachers and other staff and the answers were strikingly similar. They included the following:

- Technical skills for the job – of a very high standard. Clearly, this means they need to be excellent teachers and it almost seems too obvious to need saying. But also, for every kind of work in the school, whatever the job, the standard needs to be first-class. That way, as several leaders explained, no learner or parent would ever be able to use the work of anyone at the school as an excuse for their own underachievement. A good number of school leaders insisted on some form of practice teaching as part of the selection and appointment process, and chose not to rely on testimonials or references without such actual evidence. Such leaders tended to apply this even to senior roles such as those of head of subject, department or faculty.

- Several leaders stressed that, even where good skills existed, they would be of little use in these difficult schools without what one called 'an overriding belief in and incredibly strong commitment to these learners being able to achieve the very best they were capable of'. This had to be, not a blind faith, but a genuine belief that these learners were just as capable as others of succeeding.

- A huge determination to achieve this and the relentless drive to make sure it happens. This involved a capacity for hard work, ability to work long hours if necessary and resilience to be able to come back from setbacks that inevitably occur.

- Many leaders stressed the absolute importance of what they often informally called 'tough love'. One leader defined this in these words: 'All staff here need to have empathy rather than sympathy. They need to be able to under-stand something of what it must be like to get up each day in what can be awful circumstances, and go back to that at the end of the day. But it is no good them just feeling sorry for them – their job is to do something about it by making sure the children achieve their full potential and not let it be wrecked by those circumstances. This sometimes, in fact, often, means being strict with them, making them do things that it would be so easy to let them off because you can understand why they might not want to do it, and excuse them. Our personal motto here is "Empathy not sympathy!"'

- Because these are often difficult schools where learners come from homes where aggression, violence, neglect and abuse can occur, many leaders said it was vital to have staff who could manage learner aggression and knew how to cope with verbal abuse. They stressed the need for strong school support systems to be in place for all staff, but said that the key to staff being effective was their realising that any aggression or abuse was not intended against them personally, but was a way of hitting out against the many negat-ives in their lives. One leader said that all staff need 'thick skins, at least on display – even if in the staffroom or at home, you have a good cry about it afterwards! And I must say, you could weep for these children sometimes!'

- Whilst most successful school leaders did not want their staff to be 'soft' in their approach to managing learners, they did want to feel that everyone who worked in the school had a strong sense of social justice. Without exception, all these leaders were powerful in their personal expression of the need for social justice and believed that education could play a big part in helping to improve the situation by reducing inequalities. They therefore ideally wanted staff who shared that commitment to improving social justice. Several made the point that, whilst they could not change the system themselves, they could help people of future generations who had come through such injustices to bring about those changes. One principal said that she always asked potential new staff –'Why do you want to help children like these?' and expected to hear in their reply something about 'righting injustices', 'putting things right' or any words that indicated an awareness of the wider picture and the chance to improve it. Not all leaders had that expectation of staff; whilst they all had it themselves, some were like Thomas, a school head in the north of England, who said bluntly; 'I don't care what their motives are about society! As long as they are excellent at their job, and are prepared to work their socks off for these kids, that's good enough for me! Actions not words-that's what count!'

A Practical Suggestion

You might like to consider the following idea from Tania, an experienced school leader of a very large secondary school, in London's most deprived borough. She describes how:

> Each year, when I am appointing new staff (and it is usually at least 12 to 18 in number), I get them all in a minibus and we go for a tour of the area. We stop in all the roughest areas and I encourage them in small groups of three or four to get out and go into a shop and have a cup of tea in a local café. They get an idea of what their leaners go home to after school and what they wake up to perhaps. It is eye-opening for several of them, and they are mostly keen to talk about what they've seen – they usually talk non-stop! Ideally, I'd like to do this when people come to the school for interview for a job, but this is the next best thing.

We believe such a practice could be equally effective in schools in rural settings, where poverty and disadvantage can be just as pernicious. Being taken around a group of villages can bring home to school staff the isolation of places where some learners live. They could also see what long journeys some have to make even before the school day begins, and see for themselves how limited the basic services can be, with some small villages for example having no shops at all, and no access to wi-fi or the internet.

Tania went on to stress that her arrangement was only done with newly appointed teachers, because all her support staff such as teaching assistants came from the local area anyway and knew it well, whereas the teachers tended to live outside the school's immediate area and travelled in to work.

What will Your Style of Leadership Be?

One thing is clear from our and others' research – there is no one type of personality that is essential for successful leadership. Leaders also tended to have different styles that came naturally to them, but the following emerged as crucial in these successful schools:

- Leaders were capable of adapting their usual style to fit specific circum-stances. Possibly, according to these leaders, the slight change that was most common was that they became more relaxed as they developed in the role and, as several pointed out, they were very 'tough' at the start and slightly less so as they felt their strategies beginning to succeed.

- 'Visibility' was mentioned by every single head. Successful school leaders in these disadvantaged schools felt they had to be visible and it was vital not to be office-bound. All senior leaders had to be seen out and about around the school, in communal areas, corridors, stairways and popping into classrooms. This did not need to be done only in a supervisory manner – although that was part of the purpose – but also in a way that made them look approachable, both to students and staff. The jargon phrase here is of course 'walk the talk'.

- The other aspect was the notion of shared leadership, trying to get other staff to feel they were or could become a form of leader in their own field. This involved encouraging staff to take responsibility for their own decisions about what action needed to be taken. In the early days, most of these leaders reported how many staff continually brought problems to them to be solved and it was necessary to regularly say things such as:

  - 'What are you thinking of doing about that?' or
  - 'What do you think we should do?' and occasionally
  - 'What is it you are asking me to do about this?' and in all cases, discussing the likely or possible outcomes of any proposed actions.

What Kind of Language Should be Used?

This issue was raised by a majority of these school leaders, and in most cases, it was acknowledged as one that they had not thought much about at the start, but the importance of which they had later come to recognise. Several felt they had learned that talking to and listening to people, and the way it was done was now recognised by them as one of the most crucial of all the skills needed for success (see Slater, 2008) with these situations. The following were advocated by a majority of the leaders:

- 'Fewer speeches!' This was one leader's succinct way of expressing her lesson learned quite quickly after taking up her first principalship in a 'tough' school. She said this was so true of all the learners. 'They do not want preaching at; they prefer action!' was another of her pithy expressions. She claimed this was also true of the school staff, although several leaders felt it was important at the beginning of their first term in the school to articulate clearly to staff the vision and aims that they should all be striving for. Opinions were definitely divided on this issue!

- The language used with learners (by all staff not just leaders) needed to be far more concrete than abstract. One leader suggested that 'hammering on about "our values" was counterproductive because 'these children think you mean your values anyway, and they need to be told about and shared with in what the value means in actual behaviour' – 'demonstrable', as noted above!

- The other very simple linguistic usage highly valued by leaders was the frequent use of 'We' and comparatively little use of 'I'. This was referred to earlier and a majority of leaders stressed its importance because it suggested collaborative effort by all staff and ultimately by all at the school, including learners, rather than just an autocratic approach. As several leaders noted, the use of the first person had a powerful effect, showing that it had become personal to him/her!

Dealing with Parents and the Community

The research showed that virtually all leaders believed that the majority of parents did actually want their children to succeed at school. The ultimate argument was actually an agreement that 'Whatever the differences, we are all on his/her side; we all want the best for your child(ren), even if we disagree about how to do it'. Thus all actions and strategies needed to be based on this premise. Our earlier chapter suggested some of these specific strategies. This did not mean that aggression from parents was tolerated – the action advocated where aggression loomed was a calming-down period, and a refusal to listen to any verbal abuse. Several leaders advocated pointing out that parents needed to realise that the school was not trying to tell them how to be better parents (except when advice was specifically requested), but that certain actions would not help the children at school. All leaders noted that it was important to understand the reasons for some parents disliking school (see earlier chapters in Part One).

Several leaders advocated meeting parents off-site, although this was more common with other staff – as we note later in this chapter.

Of course, all leaders had experienced some totally unacceptable behaviour from a small number of parents, often caused by drunkenness or something similar and there were leaders who had been threatened by parents. Standing up to this tiny number was important and leaders felt it usually sent out a powerful message about what would not be tolerated. As one head teacher noted – 'It only happened to me twice in 11 years, and in both cases, it emerged that the father was a known bully in the neighbourhood and the school's reputation was enhanced in both cases. In one case, the son concerned went on to perform really well at school – while his father was in prison!'

The other advice from leaders was twofold: back your staff, *but* admit when the school has made a mistake!

Teachers and Other Staff

If you are or become a teacher, or another member of staff in a school in a greatly disadvantaged context, here are some thoughts for your consideration. The evidence seems clear that, as well as being a very good teacher in the classroom (no small consideration in the first place!), you, and all support staff in the school likewise, will need the following:

- a genuine belief that all the learners that are to be found in such schools do have the ability to succeed to the best of their individuality, and a determination and commitment to ensure that they do this

- an understanding that, whilst you have compassion for, and recognition of, some of the huge disadvantages they face, you will often need to push them hard to believe in themselves, even when this sometimes seems harsh

- a willingness to give a huge amount of energy and time to enable this to happen – with a recognition that this may be exhausting and draining, but a belief that the rewards are immense

- an ability to cope with setbacks, sometimes significant ones, and a realisation that these are part of the job and inevitable, but they can be overcome

- an ability to cope with negative behaviour and attitudes at times, through recognising that this is very rarely personally intended. This does not mean tolerating bad behaviour but being able to manage it in line with school procedures and personal professional judgement

- a commitment to one's own personal professional development through various forms, recognising that as a reflective professional there is a need to constantly develop

- an ability and willingness to accept that families and communities are a crucial part of any learner's path to progress, and that, however negative these appear at times, their role is recognised. Where such people are supportive, it is vital to work with them to help the learner, and, where they are not, to provide extra support if necessary and avoid aggravating these negative outlooks

- a keenness to work with other colleagues in every possible way so that collaboration is the norm and to assist any colleague who appears isolated, by supporting them in an appropriate way

- a willingness to work with any other school with which your own school collaborates and be open to ideas from there, as much as from in your own school

- finally, having strategies for one's own personal support out of school through whatever process or network is best suited to one's needs, and a willingness to seek help whenever it is felt to be needed

It is clear that many of these issues overlap, so that whatever role a person has in the school, the key principles and actions are similar. If we had to pick out one feature that is common to each of these schools that were so successful with learners from disadvantaged contexts, it would perhaps be the incredible sense of 'togetherness' that was evident in every one.

Summary

This chapter has attempted to:

- note some of the systemic changes that might be needed in various countries' educational procedures for the attainment gap to be eliminated
- set out, in summarising the findings from the research, principles and practical suggestions for aspiring and actual school leaders to succeed in disadvantaged schools
- suggest a few of the key qualities and abilities that teachers and other school staff should ideally have to succeed in these schools.

Finally, we would stress once again that there are no simple solutions or remedies or even good practices that can easily be transferred from one school to another. One of the strengths of education and also one of the joys of working in it is that each person you work with is unique! Each child is unique, each teacher is unique, each leader is unique – *you* are unique! Of course, this is also education's great challenge and difficulty. Each school in disadvantaged contexts is unique, as is each person it. That does not mean lessons cannot be learned from other people and other schools – they can, but which specific lessons is a matter for those undertaking the task. After all, that is why we have written this book about highly successful schools, leaders and staff! What is imperative is that in trying to apply any of these lessons learned, you pick from them what suits you and the specific school and only you know those!

References

Abbott, I. (2015) Politics and Education Policy into Practice: Conversations with Former Secretaries of State. *Journal of Educational Administration and Leadership.* Vol. 47, No. 4, 334–349

Abbott, I. and Middlewood, D. 'Schools as Communities', paper for Limpopo Education, Warwick University, 2015

Abbott, I., Middlewood, D. and Robinson, S. (2013) Prospecting for Support in a Wild Environment: Investigating a School-to-School Support System for Primary School Leaders. *School Leadership and Management.* Vol. 34, No. 5: 439–453

Abbott, I., Middlewood, D. and Robinson, S. (2013) Birmingham Pupil Premium Research Report, Birmingham, Birmingham CC

Abbott, I., Middlewood, D. and Robinson, S. (2015) It's Not Just about Value for Money: A Case Study of Values-led Implementation of the Pupil Premium in Outstanding Schools, *Management in Education*, Vol. 29, No. 4, 178–184

Abbott, I., Rathbone, M., Whitehead, P. (2013) *Education Policy.* London: Sage

Abbott, I., Rathbone, M., and Whitehead, P. (2019) *The Transformation of Teacher Education.* London: Routledge

Abdi, A. (2014) Difference, Educational Equity and Social justice in Canada: Critical Analyses in Mulcahy, D.E., Mulcahy, D.G. and Saul, R. (eds) *Education in North America*, London, Bloomsbury

Antonucci, L. (2016) *Deepening Inequality in Times of Austerity*, Bristol, Policy Press

BBC (2020) Scottish Exam Grades will be based on teacher estimates, www.bbc.com (accessed 20 August 2020)

Benn, M. (2020) England's Exam Results Fiasco has Exposed its Flawed Education System. *Guardian*, 11 August 2020

Benn, M. and Downs, J. (2016) *The Truth about Our Schools*, London, Routledge

Berners-Lee, T. (2020) Like Water, Access to the Web must be a Universal Right, *Guardian Journal*, 5 June, 1–2

Bolat, O. (2014) Turkey: A Critical Perspective on Educational Leadership and Reform, in Ivanenko, N. (ed.) *Education in Eastern Europe and Eurasia*, London, Bloomsbury, pp. 149–162

Brock, C. (2011) *Education as a Global Concern*, London, Continuum

Bull, T. (1989) Home–school Links: Family-oriented or Business-oriented? *Educational review*, Vol. 41, No. 2, 113–119

Burgess, S., Briggs, A., McConnell, B. and Slater, H. (2017) School Choice in England: Background Facts, CMPO working Party Series 06/159, Institute of Public Affairs, University of Bristol

Burnitt, M. and Gunter, H. (2013) Primary School Councils: Organisation, Composition and Headteacher Perceptions, *Management in Education*, Vol. 27, No. 2, 56–62

Bush, T. (2019) Models of Educational Leadership, in Bush, T., Bell, L. and Middlewood, D. (eds) *The Principles of Educational Leadership and Management*, London, Sage, pp. 3–18

Bush, T. and Glover, D. (2002) School Leadership: Concepts and Evidence, Nottingham, Report for the National College of School Leadership

Bush, T. and Middlewood, D. (2013) *Leading and Managing People in Education*, London, Sage

Carpenter, H., Dyson, A., Papps, I., Bragg, V., Kerr, K., Todd, L, and Lang, K. (2013) Evaluation of Pupil Premium, London, DFE

Casella, R. (2014) Demographic Change and Suburban School Policy Challenges, in Mulcahy, D.E., Mulcahy, D.F. and Saul, P. (eds) *Education in North America*, London, Bloomsbury, pp. 175–194

Crawford, C., Gregg, P., MacMillan, L., Vignoles, A. and Wyness, G. (2016) Higher Education, Career Opportunities, and Intergenerational Inequality, *Oxford Review of Economic Policy*, Vol. 32, No. 4, 553–575

Davies, B. (2006) *Leading the Strategically Focused School*, London, Paul Chapman Publishing

Darling-Hammond, L. (2007) Race, Inequality and Educational Accountability: the Irony of 'No Child Left Behind', *Race, Ethnicity and Education*, Vol. 10, No. 3, 243–260

Delisle, J. and Cooper, P. (2018) Low-Income Students at Selective Colleges: Disappearing or Holding Steady? Report for the American Enterprise Institute, July 2018

Donaldson-Feilder, E., Yarker, J. and Lewis, R. (2011) *Preventing Stress in Organisations*, Chichester, Wiley-Blackwell

Dryfoos, J., Quinn, J. and Barkin, C. (2005) *Community Schools in Action*, Oxford, Oxford University Press

Dunford, J. (2014) Using Pupil Premium Effectively: An Evidence-Based Approach to Closing the Gap, *Teaching Leaders Quarterly*, Edition 5, pp. 7–9

Dunne, M. and Gazeley, L. (2008) Teachers, Social Class, and Under-achievement, *British Journal of Sociology of Education*, Vol. 29, No. 5, 451–463

Education Endowment Foundation (2020) Impact of School Closures on the Attainment Gap: Rapid Evidence Assessment. Education Endowment Foundation: London

Faulkner, C. (2015) Experience of Principalship in Two South African High Schools in Multiply Deprived Rural Areas, EMAL, Vol. 43, No. 3, 418–432

Flutter, J. and Ruddock, J. (2004) *Consulting Pupils: What's in it for Schools?* London, Routledge

Fullan, M. (2007) *The New Meaning of Educational Change*, London, Routledge

Halsey, A., Heath, A. and Ridge, J. (1980) *Origins and Destinations: Family, Class and Education in Modern Britain*, Oxford, Clarendon Press

Harris, A. and Jones, M. (2019) Leading Schools in Challenging Circumstances, in Bush, T., Bell, L. and Middlewood, D. (2019) *Principles of Educational Leadership and Management*, London, Sage, pp. 259–273

Hascher, T. (2011) Wellbeing, in Jarvela, S. (ed) *Social and Emotional Aspects of Learning*, London, Academic Press, pp. 99–112

Haycock, K., Lynch, M, and Engle, J. (2010) Opportunity Adrift: Why our Flagship Universities are Straying from their Public Mission, Education Trust, January 2010

House of Commons Education Committee (2015) Underachievement in Education of White Working Class Children, Report of Session, London, House of Commons

House of Commons Education and Social Care Committee (2008) Mental Health Issues for Children and Young People and Provision for its Treatment

Hutchinson, J., Reader, M. and Akhal, A. (2020) Education in England: Annual Report 2020. London: Education Policy Institute

Le Grand, J. and Bartlett, W. (1993) *Quasi-markets and Social Policy*. Basingstoke: MacMillan

Lucy, W. and Phillips, D. (2000) *Confronting Suburban Decline*, Washington, DC, Island Press

McCoy (2020) Will England's Coronavirus Crisis Get Worse this Winter? *Guardian*, 13 August

Markovits, D. (2019) *The Meritocracy Trap*, London, Allen Lane

McCharen, B., Song, J. and Martens, J. (2011) School Innovation: The Mutual Impacts of Organisational Learning and Creativity. *Educational Management Administration and Leadership*, Vol. 39, No. 6, 676–694

Matsumoto, M. (2013) Conclusion. In Matsumoto, M. (ed.) *Education and Disadvantaged Children and Young People*, London, Bloomsbury

Middlewood, D. (2019) Supporting Disadvantaged Children to Raise their Attainment, in Abbott, I., Huddleston, P. and Middlewood, D. (eds) *Preparing to Teach In Secondary Schools*, London, Open University Press/McGraw-Hill Education, pp. 299–310

Middlewood, D. and Abbott, I. (2015) *Improving Professional Learning through In-house Inquiry*. Bloomsbury: London

Middlewood, D. and Abbott, I. (2017) Developing a Culture for Sustainability in Educational Organisations, in Papa, R. and Saiti, A. (eds) *Building for a Sustainable Future in Our Schools*. Springer: Switzerland

Middlewood, D. and Abbott, I. (2018) *Collaborative School Leadership*, London: Bloomsbury.

Middlewood, D. and Abbott, I. (2016) Some first steps in a development of collaborative school leadership culture in parts of rural South Africa, paper presented at Conference for School Leaders, University of Warwick

Middlewood, D., Abbott, I., Netshandama, V., and Whitehead, P. (2017) Policy Leadership, School Improvement and Staff Development in England, Tanzania and South Africa: Schools Working Together, in Miller, P. (ed.) *Cultures of Educational Leadership*. Palgrave Macmillan: London

Middlewood, D., Abbott, I. and Robinson, S. (2018) *Collaborative School Leadership*. Bloomsbury: London

Middlewood, D. and Parker, R. (2009) *Leading and Managing Extended Schools*, London, Paul Chapman Publishing

Milner, K. (2019) *It's A No-Money Day*, London, Barrington-Stoke

Monti, D. (2004) *Wannabe: Gangs in Suburbs and Schools*, Oxford and Cambridge, MA, Blackwell

Mortimore, P. (2013) *Education under Siege*, Bristol, Policy Press

NCES (2018) Annual review, www.nces.edgov/ (accessed 30 July 2020)

Nieto, S. (2003) What Keeps Teachers Going? *Educational Leadership*, Vol. 60, No. 8, 14–18

O'Donoghue, T. and Clarke, S. (2019), Educational Leadership in Post-conflict Situations, in Bush, T., Bell, L. and Middlewood, D. (eds) *The Principles of Educational Leadership and Management*, London, Sage pp. 357–371

OECD (2018) Effective Teacher Policies, Paris, OECD

OECD (2018) Equity in Education, Breaking Down Barriers to Social Mobility. Paris: OECD Publishing

OECD (2019) Education at a Glance: OECD Indicators. Paris: OECD Publishing

Ofsted (2017) Ofsted Strategy 2017–22. London: Ofsted

Ofsted (2020) Ofsted: About us. www.gov.uk (accessed 17 August 2020)

Orfield, M. (2002) *American Metro Politics: The New Suburban Reality*, Washington, DC, The Brookings Institution

Oxford University (2020) Access and Participation Plan 2020–21 to 2024–25

Patel (2020) Too many A-level Grades are Patently Wrong. *Guardian*, 15 August

Parker, R. (1997) Passion and Intuition: The Impact of Life Histories on School Leadership, Nottingham, National College for School Leadership

Parker, R. and Middlewood, D. (2013) *The Reality of School Leadership*, London: Bloomsbury

Parrish, M. (2010) *Social Work Perspectives on Human Behaviour*, Maidenhead, Open University Press

Parsons, S. and Hallam, S. (2014) Impact of Streaming on Attainment: Evidence from the Millennium Cohort Study, *Oxford Review of Education*, Vol. 40, No. 5, 567–589

Raffo, C., Dyson, A., Gunter, H., Hall, D., Jones, L, and Kalambuka, A. (2007) *Education and Poverty*, London, JRF

Reay, D. (2017) *Miseducation*, Bristol, Policy Press

Reay, D. (2012) 'We Never Get a Fair Chance: Working-class Experiences of Education in the Twenty-first Century, in Atkinson, W., Roberts, S. and Savage, M. (eds) *Class Inequality in Austerity Britain*, Basingstoke, Palgrave MacMillan

Ruddock, J. and McIntyre, D. (2007) *Improving Learning Through Consulting Pupils*, London, Routledge

Rury, J. (2014) Turning Points: Critical Periods in Educating the United States, in Mulcahy, D.E., Mulcahy, D.G. and Saul, R. (eds) *Education in North America*, London, Bloomsbury

Ryan, R. and Deci, E. (2000) Intrinsic and Extrinsic Motivation: Classic Definitions and New Developments, *Contemporary Educational Psychology*, 25, pp. 54–67

Scambler, G. and Blane, D. (2003) Inequality and Social Class, in Scambler, G. (ed) *Sociology as Applied to Medicine*, London, Saunders, pp. 107–123

Scheicher, A. (2013) Report on Impact of National Education Policies, Paris, OECD, p. 4

Seligman, M. (1979) *Helplessness: On Depression, Development and Death*, San Francisco, Freeman

Sharp, C., Nelson, J., Lucas, M., Julius, J., McCrone, T. and Sims, D. (2020) The Challenges Facing Schools and Pupils in September 2020. Slough: National Foundation for Educational Research

Smith, E. (2018) *Key Issues in Education and Social Justice*. London: Sage

Smyth, J. and Simmons P. (2017) Where is Class in the Analysis of Working-class Education?' in Smyth, J. and Simmons, P. (eds) *Education and Working-class Youth*, Basingstoke, Palgrave MacMillan, pp. 1–39

Sobel, D. (2018) *Narrowing the Attainment Gap: A Handbook for Schools*. London: Bloomsbury.

Social Mobility Commission (2018) Annual Review: section on extra-curricular activities, London, Department for Education, pp. 19–23

Social Mobility Commission (2020) What the Social Mobility Commission does, www.gov.uk (accessed 20 August 2020)

Stevenson, J. and Clegg, S. (2012) Possible Selves: Children Orienting Themselves Towards the Future, *British Educational Research Journal*, Vol. 37, No. 2, 231–246

Stinson, D. and Wager, A. (2012) *Teaching Mathematics for Social Justice*, Reston, V., National Council For Teachers of Mathematics

Sutton Trust (2020) About us, www.suttontrust.com (accessed 21 July 2020)

Teach for America (2020) What we do, https://teachforamerica.org (accessed 21 July 2020)

Thomas, D. (2008) *Cross-cultural Management: Essential Concepts* (2nd ed.), Thousand Oaks, CA, Sage

Todd, L. (2007) *Partnerships for Inclusive Education*, Abingdon, Routledge

Townsend, P. (1979) *Poverty in the United Kingdom*, Harmondsworth, Penguin Books

UNESCO (2015) The Incheon Declaration – Education 2030: towards Inclusive and Equitable Quality Education and Lifelong Learning for All. Paris: Unesco.

UNICEF (2018) Report on Unaccompanied Refugee Children and the allocation of school places, Paris, UNICEF

Vignoles, A. and Powdthavee, N. (2009) The Socio-economic Gap in University Dropouts, *B.E. Journal of Economic Analysis and Policy*, Vol. 28, No. 1, 1–36,

Vince, G. (2019) *Transcendence: How Humans Evolved*, London, Allen Lane

Wolfendale, S. (1996) The Contribution of Parents to Children's Achievements in School, in Bastiani, J. and Wolfendale, S. (eds) *Home–School Work in Britain*, London, David Fulton

Zaranko, B. (2020) Levelling up: What Might it Mean for Public Spending? London: Institute for Fiscal Studies

Index